THE PRIVILEGE OF HIS COMPANY

William Marchant

THE PRIVILEGE OF HIS COMPANY

Noël Coward Remembered

Weidenfeld and Nicolson London

First published in Great Britain by
Weidenfeld and Nicolson
11 St John's Hill London SW11

ISBN 0 297 76937 5

Printed in Great Britain by
REDWOOD BURN LIMITED
Trowbridge and Esher

For
Tabitha Parker Fondes

Acknowledgments

The author would like to express his gratitude to Mr. Paul Myers, Curator of the Theatre Collection of the New York Public Library at Lincoln Center, New York City, along with his delight and wonder at the riches to be found there and the gracious assistance of Mr. Myers's staff. Special thanks are also due to Mr. Alexander Fondes for his energies and devotion in researching the facts, figures, and the photograph by Lawrence Fried.

Foreword

My first visit to the theatre to see live actors in a dramatic entertainment was as a boy of eight, and the play was Noël Coward's *Private Lives,* with the author and Gertrude Lawrence in a cast that also included the young Laurence Olivier. It was perhaps a somewhat eccentric choice for my grandmother, who was my companion, to have made: a comedy about marital infidelity could scarcely have been thought the ideal piece with which to inaugurate a child's theatregoing (we, in fact, saw an elaborate production of *Alice In Wonderland* later the same week), but it was a happy inspiration, as it turned out, for it decided then and there, in the course of a matinee, what direction my adult life would later follow.

The economic depression of the thirties was then severely felt everywhere, and the theatrical entertainments of the day were predominantly trifles of a spun-sugar kind, confections guaranteed to sweeten the harsh taste of the ugly reality outside the theatre's walls. When I was sufficiently recovered from a long childhood illness to make monthly visits to theatres in New York, it was these diversions I liked best: the drawing-room comedies with elegantly dressed ladies sipping cocktails and delivering wickedly funny lines as if they had just sprung to mind, and the Rodgers and Hart musical shows with their catchy songs and lively dancing. The serious drama did not very much attract me at first, though I puzzled over O'Neill and Ibsen at home and wondered at their appeal for audiences.

Reading plays, or about the theatre, was almost as much fun as going to it, and the free library of the Pennsylvania town where my school days were spent was a mine of informative material. It was the decade when the words "glamour" and "star" took on a new meaning and achieved household currency; the press made instant legends out of newcomers to the scene, and the established celebrities moved in an Olympian world of luxurious ease whose activities dazzled the reader. Books about the high life by those who lived it were popular, and the first one to come to my attention was the first volume Noël Coward wrote, while still in his early thirties, about his life till then, *Present Indicative*.

Coward's progress from boy actor in the London theatre to international celebrity was self-documented in a breezy style that made good reading and encouraged me to set my sights on an objective similar to his own early one, although the kind of apprenticeship he had served in the acting profession did not attract me as the ideal steppingstone. To be able to write plays for the theatre, it was evident to me, one had to know a great deal about acting and how it was done, but the knowledge of the craft had surely been assimilated by other dramatists without their having ever set foot on a stage. Happily for me, it was a time when very fine acting was a commonplace. From the last rows of the balcony nearly every Saturday afternoon I studied and enjoyed many of the most eminent actors of the day: the incomparable Lunts, Laurette Taylor, Ina Claire, Walter Huston, and my special darling, Gertrude Lawrence.

It was the anthology of nine one-act plays Noël Coward wrote for himself and Gertrude Lawrence to act, under the umbrella title of *Tonight at 8:30,* performed in New York during the winter of 1937, that fixed my determination to write for the theatre once and for all. The brilliant variety of the three evenings that made up what survives in my memory as the most skillful demonstration of theatrical versatility I ever saw set Noël Coward apart, in my mind, from his contemporaries by the sheer nature of his accomplishment. He had written, directed and acted in all nine of the short plays. Three of them contained songs for which he had written the music and lyrics as well. He played a third-rate music-hall performer in one and provided a sample of mediocre vaudeville entertainment that was imaginatively awful. He played a middle-aged working-class victim of an unfortunate marriage, an urbane young man attempting to recapture the past, a Victorian martinet, a Harley Street psychoanalyst, a down-at-the-heels playboy. In the classic *Still Life,* which later became the film *Brief Encounter,* he was a forlorn London businessman attempting a romance with a married woman during clandestine meetings in a railway luncheonette. The total effect was somehow greater than the sum of its parts and made Coward unique. When, many years later, he came to be called "the Master" by everyone who knew him, it seemed perfectly fine and fitting to me so long as the honorific was his alone.

Yet at the time his reputation as a dramatist and even as an actor suffered somewhat from the public personality he wore: his quips and withering rejoinders were quoted so widely in the press that it was Coward the wit that the public recognized and not Coward the theatrician. It was hard to reconcile the hard-working dramatist and composer with the photographs of him in *Town and Country* and *Vogue,* portraits of a languid, impeccably tailored man with a high forehead and a look of faintly amused disapproval. There was a great deal of contradictory gossip, too, and his membership in the fashionable world on both sides of the Atlantic made him seem frivolous and dilettantish rather than serious and dedicated to his craft. The name Noël Coward called to mind an image of an Englishman in a silk dressing gown, wreathed in clouds of cigarette smoke, who played the piano nicely and said bitchy things, and who sometimes, to keep from being bored, acted in plays he wrote for himself. All the hearsay about him tantalized me considerably throughout my adolescence and later university days, when I studied playwriting technique and the history of the drama, and my admiration for him survived a fundamental alteration in my growing taste for more substantial theatrical fare. My ambitions were specific: I was going to write plays, and eventually one of them would be performed professionally, and I would move easily among the Broadway theatrical community and come to know all its people well, and inevitably one of them would be Noël Coward.

These dreams did not become a reality until I was twenty-seven years old, and when I met Noël Coward at last, the flesh-and-blood reality of him contradicted everything I had ever read or heard.

To begin with, his offstage personality differed radically from what I judged the man underneath the actor to be like: the clipped, rapid speech was the same and the silken voice identical, but the words were different. The flippancy and archness were replaced by a manner that was entirely sober, and his concentration on what others were saying gave him a look of intensity unlike that of anyone I have ever known. When he smiled it was like a benediction, and his laughter was an announcement of approval. When we met he had a way of showing great concern for my comfort that produced instant relaxation: he seemed at pains to make me feel that our meeting was the most natural and everyday thing in the world, as if we had known each other always but had not met often in the recent past. The understandable awe in which I held him was dissipated at once. I was made to understand that we were on equal footing, co-workers in a profession whose mysterious nature needed continual scrupulous attention and examination if we were to continue in it. Implicit in this understanding was the suggestion that he found me extremely gifted and yet oddly wasteful of these gifts. He offered fatherly advice, not only about my writing but about what he called my "modus vivendi," the practical side of how and where I lived and what I did with my time. The paternal stance he assumed with me soon after we first shook hands continued throughout the rest of his life, and twenty-three years later there had been no change; I still felt that, through some eccentric process of adoption, I was his son as well as his friend.

He asked nothing of me other than that I consider his wisdom carefully. Years would elapse between our meetings, sometimes three or four, when he was away somewhere or I was in some remote corner of Europe, but our encounters never had about them a sense of recommencement. They always seemed to continue precisely where they left off, like an unfinished sentence suddenly provided with its completed thought before the next one can begin.

If relationships could be measured by the quantity of hours they consumed, mine with Nöel Coward would add up to an unimpressive figure, but it was precisely the infrequency of our meetings and the rapport we enjoyed when they did occur that gave to them such an intensity and, to me, such pleasure. So very many things managed to crowd themselves into a meeting of a few hours: news exchanged, works-in-progress discussed, wise counsel offered, voyages suggested, fond reminiscences told and retold. In hindsight I must acknowledge that I was never an intimate friend of his, and those who were, those who shared his various residences with him or saw him daily, and who often seemed like satellites in perpetual revolution about a central sun, I knew only very casually. Yet we all had one affection in common that elevated us to membership in the same consistory, and that was a reverential love for a man we all knew to be very much out of the ordinary.

Friendships are popularly supposed to grow, to deteriorate, or at least to show some evidence of change. Mine with Noël Coward observed no such traditional alterations; it was always constant, highly personal, and refreshing. It was perhaps the refreshment that I felt most strongly after a few hours spent in his company, a feeling of being charged with energy and a strong sense of renewed purpose.

What I knew of him, and loved and admired in him, was the Noël Coward who was the master of whatever he attempted, and it was this side of him that made up his self-presentation. His origins were certainly humble, and he frequently enjoyed reminding people exactly how humble they had been, but his bearing and demeanor were always those of a gentleman and sometimes even of a prince. To me he seemed always to be in such perfect control of the moment that no situation was ever so unforeseen that it might become unmanageable. What I knew of him derived principally from what he said, and what he said of himself by way of description, and what he wished to convey to others of his experience and intellect for their benefit or merely their amusement.

I am no diarist, and I have not the discipline of keeping, as many writers do, journals of recorded personal history, but soon after I met Noël for the first time (in fact, the second day) I began to jot down in a haphazard fashion and in a kind of personal shorthand the things he said that I wanted to remember. When, soon after he died, I unearthed accordion folders from a file cabinet and found the backs of envelopes, lined yellow foolscap pages, pocket diaries from a decade ago, all kinds of odds and ends of paper with notations in ink and pencil, some illegible, some too cryptic to decipher, the voice behind those recorded words was so insistent that my task was clear.

At that stage, of course, the assembled words needed a coherence and a chronology. But I found that the notes insisted upon their own order, and what follows is the result: a memoir so personal that it might be at variance with the recollections of others, a memory only of time spent with Noël Coward and the great sense of occasion each encounter unfailingly provided. I felt no urge to summarize, add up or interpret in the hindsightful way that is now fashionable in published reminiscences. For me there was never anything to sum up: the elements of the equation were sufficient joy to contemplate.

Sometimes, of course, one could observe puzzling contradictions in the man, but they only made him, to my mind, more of what the English call an "original." He was, as John Osborne has said, his own greatest invention.

1

The summer of 1950 was said to be the hottest summer within American memories. The flatland surrounding Westport, Connecticut, seemed to magnetize the heat, and the lawns were parched, strawlike implantations that no sprinkler systems could make green; early July had an autumnal look and the crickets chirped without interruption in the old elms that decorated the garden of Jack Wilson's house near Fairfield, promising no relief from the humidity for days to come, no rainfall, no breeze from the Sound, nothing but the staleness of uncirculated air and the monotonous fragrance of early hay and alfalfa that infused it. Hydrangea blossoms the size of basketballs drooped lamentably in the continuous glare. The pool at the Wilsons' had a phosphorescent surface

originally contained in bottles of suntan oil, and the decorative group of swimmers convened there one Saturday afternoon in the cruel sun baked themselves under its rays like basted fowls in an oven.

Allergic to direct sunlight since childhood, I was stretched out on a canvas garden chaise in the shade of an awning attached to the roof of the changing rooms. Accustomed, also since childhood, to sleeping an hour or so in midafternoon, I dozed slightly behind steaming sunglasses.

"Are you the author?" I heard a voice behind me. "Or are you merely trying to get attention by upstaging everyone else?"

He was a mere silhouette against the western sky, but the voice was unmistakably Noël Coward's. I squinted. I had the impression of a navy blue pullover, white duck trousers and espadrilles. A gold watchband gleamed. I sat up. It was some trick of light, perhaps, or else a gifted mimic had stopped by for a swim. To my knowledge, Noël Coward wasn't even in the Western Hemisphere.

"I'm the only author present," I said as he moved around into the shadow and I could see him plainly. "Or *was,*" I added hurriedly, "until now."

"Aren't you *very* young," he asked, "to embark on such a strenuous life?"

As I remember, I had no answer for that, and welcomed the sight of Jack Wilson, lithe and bronze and dripping wet, padding across the rough concrete terrace to introduce us properly. He offered glasses of the "house" iced tea, drinks in tall frosted containers like something on a drugstore counter, heavily laced with brandy and lime juice.

"That's a very serious drink," said Noël, "for one so young."

My baby face and military cadet haircut had often served me

badly in mature company, especially in the Army Air Force during World War II, and I had only weeks before been asked for proof of my age when ordering a glass of beer in a bar. Yet I was twenty-seven years old and was perfectly able to hold my liquor with the best of them. I accepted one of the Wilson tea concoctions almost defiantly. The idea that my appearance created an impression of callowness was not new to me, but in that environment it was unsettling, and I wondered what I might do to offset it. Perhaps Noël discerned something of this self-consciousness, for he immediately adopted a manner that was tutorial and teasing.

I lit a cigarette. He elevated his eyebrows in an expression of mock astonishment. Obviously I was also too young to smoke.

"Have you heard about the youth implantations of the Russian Dr. Bogomoletz?" he asked.

"Something about the liver of an unborn ewe, or kid, or something?"

He sat down, half in the sun and half in shadow, nodded and took his drink in rapid, tiny sips. "It is evident that, in your case at least, they have performed wonders." Jack laughed, poured out some of the iced tea for himself, and wandered away to his other guests.

"Or else I should never believe that you had written that play," Noël continued.

The first play I had written was then rehearsing under Jack Wilson's direction, to be performed in a week's time at the Westport Country Playhouse, of which Jack was part owner. "My first thought was that some distinguished playwright is experimenting with a new and unconventional form and hopes to remain incognito until the play has bowled everyone over, whereupon he will emerge from his disguise and say that you have been fronting for him."

It was fanciful, and funny, and there was praise implicit in it, and I laughed. "Which distinguished playwright?" I asked.

"So it *is* true!" he exclaimed. "I knew it! Why, Maxwell Anderson, obviously. Please tell him for me that it is quite the best thing he's ever done."

In this way I learned that he had read the play. A day earlier Jack had received a cablegram I was shown later. "Lonely as a cloud and arriving Fairfield noontime tomorrow." In fact Noël had arrived in midafternoon, retired instantly to the bedroom assigned to him and spent the next few hours with my script.

There is no heady thrill to compare with that enjoyed by a fledgling dramatist when an acknowledged master of the craft praises his work; chills of pleasure ripple between the shoulder-blades, the mouth goes dry with excitement, and a pleasurable faintness takes hold of the brain. Surely he had himself experienced a similar euphoria in 1919 when his first play caused such a stir of enthusiasm among the London theatrical community and Bernard Shaw wrote him an uncharacteristic letter of encouragement. But if he was enjoying my enjoyment of the moment he made no sign to suggest it.

He wanted to talk about it at once. He made it seem like a matter of great urgency, and it was only later, when the highly technical nature of the conversation that followed managed to dissipate some of the excitement I was feeling, that I realized why he attached so much importance to what was in reality only a week's trial run in a summer stock theatre. Jack, as John C. Wilson, was then riding the crest of a wave that had begun with the production of *Kiss Me, Kate* and steepened with the direction of *Gentlemen Prefer Blondes*, two monumental Broadway successes that had made him the most sought-after director in the American theatre. Previously he had been known only as Noël Coward's business manager, and later the producer of his plays in their New York incarnations. Noël had for years been urging Jack to try his hand at more substantial stuff, at serious American plays by new American writers, and my play was the first one to have aroused Jack's interest sufficiently to produce it, however cautiously and tentatively, on a stage.

Noël suggested we go inside the house and take our drinks with us. I scrambled out of the garden chaise eagerly, and Noël waved to Madame Valentina, on the other side of the pool, vocally admiring her tan as we passed her.

The library of the Wilson house was efficiently refrigerated and dark, comfortably furnished with sofas and wing chairs covered in black and white chintz; it was eminently suited to quiet, professional conferences and play-reading. A gunmetal gray manuscript folder lay open on a footstool, and the pages of my play were dog-eared and marked with notations at the top and bottom in brown ink. Noël sat down and leaned over the script, turning to the title page and looking at it with a studious frown. I worried that he didn't like the title, *Within a Glass Bell.*

"No," he confirmed. "Well, that can wait till later on. First let me ask a few questions, and the particulars will follow in due course. I take it the story is only partly autobiographical?"

The play was a drama set in a beautifully appointed apartment on the East Side of New York City, hung from floor to ceiling with valuable pictures of the neo-Surrealist school and framed sketches of ballet costumes and scenery by Bérard, Tchelitchew and Berman. The disposition of these pictures and certain other ornaments to correct the impoverishment of the owners was the burden of much of the play's action; the treasures had taken on a meaning like that of the spoils of Poynton in the Henry James novel: they represented to the woman who had bought them the joys of her

expatriate youth in Europe and to her unhappy son the means of
a financial salvation that would effect his release from the hothouse
atmosphere of the fatherless home he shared with her. At a time
when the postwar displaced persons of Europe were the daily
subject of newspaper editorials and official concern, the characters
I had written were emotionally displaced, longing to be on the
Riviera or in Normandy at a fashionable watering place and confi-
dent that the clock's hands might be reversed to a happier and
more carefree time. These dreams were pungently described in
repetition throughout the play like recurring melodies, and the
ambient, somewhat seedy splendor gave the story a threat of im-
pending doom that was unspoken but never very far from the
characters' thoughts.

Most first plays, it seems, tend to have a strong autobiographical etiology, and it was then the prevailing fashion to see every
unhappy young man in the work of a new playwright as a partially
disguised self-portrait. The hero of my play was totally unlike me
in every way and his mother a very different kind of woman from
my own, and I thought it would be best to tell Mr. Coward that right
away. He seemed surprised.

"It is so deeply felt that I thought you must have experienced
it," he said. "If it isn't about *you,* what made you write it?"

I told him of a young man I had gone to school with, a frail
and sickly person who had been dragged from one European capital to another since his early childhood by an extravagant mother
who squandered a considerable fortune on underwriting everything from indigent painters to failing ballet companies. Their dis-
placement in New York following the war's outbreak, keeping to
themselves and rarely venturing out-of-doors, chattering intermi-
nably about the dear, dead days abroad, had saddened and moved

me deeply, and their folly was the subject of the play he had just read.

"The details are so right," he said. "I thought they must have been the details of your own inconsiderable past. The people are presented with real affection, whereas they could so easily be merely rather silly and tiresome. Or unpleasant, which would be fatal. There is something about these people you admire, isn't there?"

I nodded. I wondered, though, if I could identify the object of my admiration. I tried to express it simply.

"It's their *taste*, I think."

He raised his eyebrows. "Not their manners?"

"I don't think I know enough about manners."

"No, because the woman, Mary, expresses herself rather indelicately from time to time, and at first I thought it was out of character for her, but I do see you are trying to express something in her nature that she herself would be the last to recognize. Now, who is playing her? Mildred Dunnock? Yes, an astonishingly fine actress, and exactly the right *temperament*. Superb in *Death of a Salesman*. Won't it be nice to see her get out of all those drab clothes?"

He was being seductive, wooing me to relax and sit with him as an equal. I never knew anyone more accomplished at this social necessity than Noël: describing it once to a lady who possessed the same ability in abundance, I asked her to put a name on it. She shrugged and said, "Charm."

Then he commenced to look through the manuscript, page by page, to read the notes he had made in brown ink. The silence was prolonged, and I began to be uncomfortable. I rattled the ice in my glass, and he looked up. "Make yourself another drink. And make me one, too, if you will. That jug on the drinks table is full of this same stuff, isn't it?"

He continued to be absorbed in the script, turning the pages back and forth, seemingly reading and rereading one scene over and over, removing his eyeglasses to stare off into a corner as if he had been reminded of something that troubled him, and then put them back on again.

"Do you know Jed Harris?" he asked.

"No."

"He refuses to read stage directions. Did you know that?"

"No," I said again.

"Someone once asked him what his understanding would be of the end of *Hedda Gabler* if he didn't read the direction about her shooting herself with the pistol, and he said that he supposed he would simply wonder why she had stopped talking."

He tapped the script with his forefinger. "This is a curious habit, and very surprising in one so young. There are so many stage directions, they must make up half the text! Have you ever directed a play?"

I hadn't, and I said so.

"Do you *want* to?"

"One day, maybe. I'll know I'm ready when the time comes."

"Decades from now, I trust. Do you really see the actors following all these specific moves? 'She rests her hand on the back of the chair and then looks at it to see if it might be dusty.' Now, why does she do that? And, more to the point, *does* she do it? Does Mildred Dunnock do it where it is indicated?"

"No," said I. "Most of the stage directions went by the wayside."

"Well, of course she doesn't. *Do* keep it simple. It makes actors worry, poor things, to see something like that and not feel it to be right and then wonder if the author had some particular meaning in mind that they have failed, in their charmed innocence, to perceive. I don't know where you can have picked up this habit."

I hurried to explain. George Kelly, one of America's greatest if most unappreciated and consequently neglected playwrights, had lectured me at some length on the need to know, down to the most minute movement, exactly what each actor was engaged in doing physically at a given moment. He held that writers who exhibited little concern for this important element of stagecraft had nobody to thank but themselves when their plays were staged haphazardly by someone else and that many a worthy work had failed because of this neglect, that a watchful regard for how a play moved on its feet decreed the length of its speeches and even of its scenes. I had slavishly followed his instructions, only to discover that my knowledge of what actors need to motivate a movement from a chair to a window or to pour sherry into a glass was insufficient to the principle of getting everything down on paper like notations for a ballet. But I protested that, in my view, the Kelly dictum was sound.

At the mention of the Kelly name, Noël nodded and said, "You are talking about the playwright's playwright."

I had heard actors described as "the actor's actor," a term often used in reference to the Lunts and even to Noël himself, but never a writer as having that special quality that made him most appreciated by others of his profession.

"George is quite unique, and knows more about the theatre than dozens of others all lumped into one, and quite frankly I esteem him more than O'Neill or anybody else living, with the exception of Bernard Shaw, who holds similiar views to George's. You will notice, however, that Shaw writes a stage direction only when the text would be unclear without it. And you will frequently hear actors say when they are appearing in some Shaw play or other that a stage direction by him can in no circumstances be violated. That if you do something other than what Shaw specifically instructed, you are in dire trouble and find yourself wandering all over the place like something without a head.

"Now, it is not," he went on, with a pause to measure his words, "it is not absolutely *dangerous* for someone like you to listen to every word that George Kelly is kind enough to tell you. We all have a lot to learn from him. He used to lecture me far into the night when I first came to America. But it must be borne in mind that George is first of all an *actor,* with an almost historical understanding of comedy which he learned from his brother and from his own vast experience in vaudeville, and there is no substitute whatsoever for that kind of experience in knowing how to write plays. Then, too, George always directs his own plays. Very few authors are good at this nowadays, sad to say. He has acted out every scene down to the last little nuance before the actors ever come to the first day's rehearsal. He sometimes says he wouldn't know how long a speech should be until he knew how many steps it was from the desk to the chair and so forth and how many words would be needed to accommodate the movement. And I believe him. That is his own highly individualistic technique and produces those magnificent plays of his, of which there are all too few. You show great perception to admire him.

"But to follow his example without digesting it and understanding the *why* of it is going to result in a copy of his manner, and I shouldn't do that if I were you. Everything about him is uniquely his, his rhythm and his speed. Not even Shaw writes women as well as George does. The last thing he wrote for Ina

Claire, *The Fatal Weakness,* was sheer bliss. There's never been a character like her in all the history of drama.

"Another side of this worth mentioning is what actors think when confronted with the tidy little cages George designs for them. I have known some very fine actresses who resented bitterly that all their work had been done for them beforehand. Of course he has his devotees among them, all of whom work for him constantly because they understand him and his methods."

He set aside the script then and got up to pace the room, rattling some coins in his pocket. Watching him on the stage, I had always been struck by the way he moved, his lower body seeming to be independent of the top. His method of locomotion had a kind of boatlike grace, a gliding forward unlike that of any other person I had ever seen. He stopped to glance down at a copy of *Vogue* on a table and waited a little before continuing.

"Would you say that this play has a theme? Does it illustrate for you some particular moral? Or didn't you have anything like that in mind when you wrote it?"

"If it says anything, I guess it's that one cannot go on living in the past and that one has to keep up with social change if one is going to survive."

"And is that true?" His look was searching.

He made me feel that perhaps it wasn't, that my youth and limited experience had not prepared me to make such a sweeping statement, that I was posturing in some way and that the play was evidence of it.

"The war brought about an enormous change in everything, and much of it I deplore," he went on. "I refuse categorically to acknowledge that anything is different, even when it stares me in the face. In your view, does that make me prehistoric?"

I told him about my grandmother and her friends, who adhered to the fashions and customs of Edwardian times even when World War II was in progress; it had made them figures of fun in the community where they lived. They wore high-button shoes until the day when no bootmaker remembered how to make them.

"You must put *them* in a play one day. Did they live in the South?"

"No, in Pennsylvania."

"Because there's rather too much about the South nowadays. Every book you pick up is set in the Carolinas. But this play of yours is a side of New York I don't know at all. I didn't know there *were* any Chekhov people living in New York—other than the White Russians."

"Chekhov people?" I repeated. "How are they Chekhov people?"

"In the sense that they are living in the past, as Mme. Ranevskaya does, as you say your booted grandmother did, as do so many of the Chekhov characters who yearn to go away somewhere else where everything will turn out to be equally bad for them once they get there. *You* know. Chekhov people."

My reply could only be defensive. He had spoken of imitating George Kelly's manner; it was possible he was saying that Chekhov had been a similar model. "I don't think I'm the only writer today who owes a debt to Chekhov." I looked him squarely in the eye. "American-Chekhov, I call it. His plays have influenced the American theatre very strongly. New writers need models. Didn't they always?"

"When I was starting out, Chekhov was very little known. But I had my own models, my own masters; and some of my early plays reveal my admiration for Pinero and certainly the drawing-room comedies of Maugham. Do you know my play *The Vortex?*

Yes, of course you do. The situation in it is very different, but there is a mother-and-son relationship there that suggests an explicit, if inactive, incestuous connection, and I find more than a mere suggestion of a similar thing in *Within a Glass Bell*. You have done it most subtly and cleverly and, I think, quite inoffensively. Whereas that side of *The Vortex* had an almost sinister aspect and made many members of the audience uncomfortable. Nowadays it doesn't matter. My early play *Easy Virtue* was a kind of turn-around of a theme in Pinero. I think all early work inevitably shows the influence of other, older dramatists, and I see nothing wrong in it, so long as it does not come right down to slavish imitation."

He strode over to a table in one corner where there was an early photograph of him in a silver frame, made at a time when seemingly every likeness of him included a cigarette between his fingers with spirals of smoke rising from it.

"Of course, this is the most ambitious thing Jack has ever undertaken. I have been at him for years to do something with a bit more substance, a bit more character. Your play seems exactly right for his first plunge into the *drama,* but I want to be sure that it is. I want to be sure that it is as right as it can ever be, which is why we are having this talk *now* and not at some future time, for *your* sake as well as his. Jack needs a great deal of encouragement to keep up his self-confidence. You may not realize what a great step it is for him to put this play on, but it *is* one, all the same."

I often thought back to these words in later years. They synthesized so neatly the elements of our friendship, setting down the ground rules then and there: he was Jack's friend; he was deeply committed to Jack's progress, as he was to that of all those he knew and loved; as an instrument of Jack's progress my play must be accorded the most scrupulous attention; I was new at the game, Noël was an old hand at it. If I could benefit from his tutelage, I too might have a friend committed to my own progress in the years to come. He assumed the position of a surrogate parent; I fell into the role of surrogate son easily.

"I am delighted," he continued, "that he has chosen to do it, and chosen to do it this way, here in Westport. The play is both delicate and very strong, and it needs to be seen in just such a way, without the overwhelming pressure of a Broadway opening night ahead of one and all that frantic rewriting that goes on. But you haven't been exposed to that sort of thing before, have you? It will come, it will come. What pleases me most for Jack is that it is such a distinct change of pace for him."

"Well," I said in a confidential way, "when my agent told me Jack wanted to produce the play, I said, 'What in the world in it interests him? The fact that its setting is on Sutton Place?' "

He was not amused. "There is a great distinction between humor and sheer nastiness," he said, and took out another cigarette.

I stammered something. I know I blushed. He made a little gesture I came to recognize years later as his substitute for a shrug.

"The tendency to see Jack only as a man of fashion is widespread, and wrong. Sutton Place and that paneled drawing room in there are not at all expressive of Jack, only of a taste for opulent refinement. Never forget that he is a boy from Trenton, New Jersey. Or that *I* was born in Teddington, Middlesex. Has Jack not told you how I characterize him? As a man with his head in the clouds and his feet planted squarely in the box office."

We talked specifics for about an hour. He found a joke to be feeble and urged me to do better; a scene at the end wanted foreshortening in the interests of pace; a speech of the mother's was not only too long but a "mouthful." Soon a great blast of sound in the distance startled us both. I explained that it was a regular

Saturday afternoon occurrence, emanating from the Westport fire-house and signaling the end of the workweek. He seemed relieved to hear it.

"We should go out now. But I want to mention this rubric on the title page."

It was then, and often still is, the custom for a producer to affix his name and address at the lower righthand corner of the title page under the words "Property of." Noël pointed to the place on my manuscript where Jack's name appeared in this way.

"It is *not* his property. It is yours."

"It's the custom," I said. "He paid out five hundred dollars option money, and he has the exclusive right to produce it for the time being. So it's his property."

"It is *not,*" Noël insisted. "Take a look at that cigarette box on the table there. Read the lid and then open it."

I was not in those days familiar with silversmiths' hallmarks or the unique design of the box that identified it as having come from only one jewelry establishment in the world, Garrard's of Regent Street, London, but I picked it up carefully and read the lid as instructed. "Property of John C. Wilson," it said. I opened the lid. Engraved on the other side in the same lettering was the legend, "Property of Noël Coward."

I laughed. "Did you give this to him?"

He nodded, with a wise smile, and we made our way back to the swimming party. Hot fingers of sunlight between lengthening shadows made a pretty pattern on the flagstones, and a faint breeze from the east brought with it a summertime fragrance that, for a change, did not smell of alfalfa. The company originally gathered there since luncheon, weekend guests and friends from a neighboring town, had been augmented with others, guests in other houses nearby. There was Margaret Case, an editor at *Vogue* whose father had owned the Algonquin Hotel and initiated the legendary Round Table at the rear of its lobby; her credentials were excellent in other respects as well. The bikini had only recently inaugurated itself as acceptable swimming attire in secluded environments among safe company, and Madame Valentina, who dressed Lynn Fontanne so exquisitely and thoroughly for the stage that often her hands and face were all that one could see of her, clutched the top half of hers to her bosom demurely, lest it come obscenely apart. As slim as a lizard or a fashion drawing by Vertès, she stretched her arm out to Noël to come and sit with her and invited him to gossip; she hadn't heard anything new in so long. But he was not at her immediate bidding, and we went instead to say hello to others: to Jane Bowles, then rewriting *In the Summerhouse* for the third time, and to Herman Levin, the producer of *Gentlemen Prefer Blondes,* who cannily assumed that Noël's surprise appearance on the scene had a professional rather than a social reason and asked at once what it might be. We were not to learn until the following morning's *New York Times* arrived that he had agreed to play opposite Gertrude Lawrence in the Rodgers and Hammerstein operetta based on *Anna and the King of Siam,* then still without a title. The "agreement" was a press agent's fantasy, the management of the projected musical refusing to believe that Noël's long-established rule of playing a role for three months only was inviolable. It was thought that the character of the King, so ideally suited to him, and the exceptional quality of the music and lyrics would persuade him to sign a contract for at least a year, anything less being unthinkable from a commercial standpoint. However, the three-month rule held, one of its happy results being the emergence of Yul Brynner as the King, an inspired bit of casting that was the commencement of a long career.

But Noël was vague about his theatrical plans and evasive in talking with Levin. He hummed a little tune I didn't know as we moved together around the pool and he greeted old friends; for years afterwards I wondered if it had been one of his own invention that was never recorded on music paper, for throughout the evening and even two days later he would hum it with a quizzical expression as if trying to identify it or give it a name.

We sat at the feet of Natasha Wilson, born a Russian princess and married to Jack, while they talked of London-based friends, of Lorn Lorraine, Noël's secretary; of Hugh Beaumont, their beloved "Binkie," the West End producer; of Noël's mother's flat in Eaton Square. Mrs. Wilson had seen a summer stock performance of *Blithe Spirit* at Westport some weeks before in which a noted American actor had played the central role in such an extravagant fashion she had turned pale with rage. "He's *such* a ham," she said.

Noël shook his head. "More a vegetarian, I'd say."

Howard, the English butler, wheeled a trolley towards us and served drinks from it, cautioning me that even the late afternoon sun was strong and that I ought to go and sit under an umbrella.

Noël looked at me with disbelief. "Heliophobia?" he asked, making it sound like some fearful contagion. My allergy to direct sunlight had been the subject of sincere dismay among the assembly all afternoon, and I was more than a little tired of it, feeling that I had committed some social blunder that would guarantee my not being invited again. "Go and sit down over there at once, dear boy, and don't take chances."

It was the first time I had heard "dear boy." That it had become, along with "dear girl," nearly as much Noël's exclusive property as "darling" was Tallulah Bankhead's was unknown to me, and I felt with a sudden rush of pleasure that I had been accepted for membership in a very exclusive club whose other members were the great and gifted of two continents. The count-less times I was to hear it throughout the next two decades never diminished the joy, and often revived it, of hearing it for the first time. That practically everyone else he worked with, or saw fre-quently, was also a "dear boy" or a "dear girl" never mattered to me; its first application to someone he had known for a mere two hours was an honorific to be treasured, repeated and remembered. I went obediently to the other side of the pool and sat under the awning.

At dinner that evening he sat to the right of Natasha Wilson and held the dozen diners in a thrall of delight as he distributed his theatrical and social notes-from-all-over among them, barely paus-ing for a mouthful of cold soup or a bite of veal as the nimble mind ran faster than the rapid tongue, and the only interruption was the laughter and the kind of coughing it produces. At last I was able to hear personally what had only ever come to me secondhand: the anecdotes, the machine-gun responses impeccably quoted but never impeccably reproduced, the trenchant remark that could destroy a reputation or elevate to instant celebrity an obscure talent. Jack Wilson had said that a time would come, during that very year, when I would hear it for myself, and had promised I would be astonished. Astonishment was too mild a word for it; what I felt was a kind of wonder, that a single human being could produce such joy among his listeners. Madame Valentina, who has the same birthday I have and on the few occasions when I have seen her has always displayed as if by some arcane power the seeming ability to read my thoughts, turned to me to ask if it was the first time I had met Noël. I said it was. "Now," she said, in her vodka voice, "you know what it is like, the pleasure of his company."

"I think," I said, "it should be called the 'privilege' of his company."

2

The following day, Sunday, Noël was off to distant parts to hear the music of what would later be called *The King and I,* and returned in the baking sun to refresh himself in the pool and amuse the other swimmers with aquatic impersonations of absent friends. He dove under, surfaced, with hands demurely cupped over the two sides of his chest. He looked about in alarm and said, in a fair approximation of Tallulah Bankhead's voice, "Is Herman Levin out here? He mustn't see me in the nude, darling!"

One of the weekend guests was a lady from Massachusetts with an old name and a powerful position on a Boston newspaper: she was its drama critic. Noël swam the length of the pool to join her where she sat in a polka-dot rubberized bathing costume that had been designed to look like something the infant Shirley Temple might have worn when she tap-danced with Bill Robinson. Noël stopped at the end of the pool, shook the water from his head and shoulders and prepared to climb out to join her briefly. She was staring into the western sky and digging with a manicured forefinger into her right nostril in such a way that it was possible she had found an uninterrupted passage to her brain. I sat nearby, paging through a local newspaper, looking for an advertisement of the attractions at the Westport playhouse. The lady continued the exploration of her nasal cavity. I looked át Noël and he returned the glance. "When you reach the bridge," he said directly to her, "I do hope you will wave good-bye to us!" With that, he submerged again, and soon climbed out at the other end of the pool.

The next morning, in an upstairs room of the Westport Y.M.C.A. where *Within a Glass Bell* was entering its final week of rehearsals, Noël and I watched the second act of my play while he made notes and whispered comments in my ear as the actors struggled with their lines and moves. The heat was already oppressive, though the hour was early, and flies buzzed in the stale air of a room that had been locked drum-tight throughout the preceding weekend; folding metal chairs creaked as their occupants shifted their weight in them. Charles Bowden, today an eminent Broadway producer, was the stage manager, superbly trained during his long association with the Lunts in the same capacity; it was he who settled Noël into a deep armchair when his discomfort became too apparent. Jack Wilson was nowhere in evidence.

"Is Jack often not on time?" Noël whispered to me.

"He says he never gets up until the crack of noon," I said.

"Then he should call rehearsals for after lunch."

Mildred Dunnock, as the mother, was having difficulty with her lines at the beginning of the act and had expressed to me earlier her suspicion that there was something wrong with their sequence; they were the only speeches that gave her trouble to memorize in what was a very long part, and, as a quick study, her experience had always been that lines that were hard for her to learn were lines that were in some way out of place. She stopped to consult her script and scratched at her scalp with a lead pencil, then turned sharply to me and said, "Let me try something to see how you like it."

"I hate suggestions," Noël said under his breath.

"What I'd like to do," Miss Dunnock went on, "is save the speech about the ferns and the rainy weather until I've shaken his hand. That way I can do it as if I were covering up the social embarrassment of seeing him again, here, after so many years. May I try that?"

I said I wished she would, and the scene was replayed from her entrance. It certainly was better, and she was clearly more comfortable doing it that way. I approved the change, and the scripts were altered in pencil to accommodate it.

Miss Dunnock works slowly and methodically, never hastily settling for a way of doing something because it comes easily to her; her intelligence guides her to explore the possibilities of a role tentatively and even haltingly, often giving the impression that she has personal misgivings about having accepted it. An approach of this kind may be familiar to dramatists with a number of plays behind them and—perhaps—even welcome. To my way of thinking, the neophyte who has not watched "method" actors develop a characterization can only suffer agonizing days and sleepless nights when he has been exposed to their rehearsing his play for the first time. Certainly I felt that something had gone terribly wrong during the previous week, that perhaps all the wrong actors had been chosen, that the play itself was bad, dull and undramatic, and that the actors were rummaging about in the text for some semblance of truth and meaning that might rescue it from its extraordinary mediocrity. There had been moments when something very nearly exciting had emerged from the days of numbing repetition, moments that allowed my hopes to run high. I know now, but did not then, that good days and bad days follow upon one another in quick succession, and the summit of delight after an excellent rehearsal becomes the bottom of gloom the next day when all is uncertainty and forgetfulness.

That morning, once the suspect speeches had been transposed, was a good one. There had been those whose counsel was that Miss Dunnock could not convincingly portray a woman of fashion or elegance. The image they retained of her was that of the down-at-heels wife in *Death of a Salesman* and the Piney Woods mother of the Hubbard clan in *Another Part of the Forest*. Yet I had seen her during the war in a Philip Barry drawing-room comedy, dressed to the nines and hung with stage diamonds, playing a wicked actress with style and grace, and I was waiting for her to display some of the same thing in the character I had written. Until that morning, shuffling about in flat shoes and a loose-fitting cotton dress, she had exhibited little beyond sweetness and sincerity and a kind of weary lack of energy that worried me considerably. Someone had said that she was exhausted after her long engagement in Arthur Miller's play. Others said that it was impossible to concentrate in such a heat wave and that it was nearly incredible that the actors could rehearse at all. Yet, touching at her brow with a crumpled handkerchief all the while and drying her palms with it from time to time, Miss Dunnock that morning became a *femme du monde,* a denizen of the Paris faubourgs, a silly pussycat with a formal manner and a man-eating tigress with a giddy one. Humid as it was, she created coolness in the envelope of air surrounding her, and Noël beamed with approval on the proceedings. I felt then, and still feel, that his presence there was the cause of it, that some sense of esteem for herself and a beyond-the-call-of-duty professionalism made her reach forward and upward to give the kind of performance she later gave before audiences.

At one point she had been directed to kneel beside a chair, embracing her son's knees and beseeching him to listen to reason, to reason as she so impractically perceived it, and the moment she did so I heard Noël murmur a disapproval. I asked him what was wrong.

"Old-fashioned," he said, as quietly as he could, and Miss Dunnock flashed a look in our direction.

The act did not come to an end, as two of the actors involved in the last scene had not been summoned until after the lunch break, but was stopped and replayed from its beginning. The second run was even better, and the young actor who played Miss Dunnock's son took on some of her own airy lightness and humor, so that the longest of their scenes together, always in danger of seeming overextended, played rapidly and well. The pleasure at the way it was going swept the room like a contagion, and when the lunch break was announced, Noël rose and went directly to Miss Dunnock to say something in admiration.

"Yes," she said, with a tired smile. "It's beginning to feel right now. I don't know why, but it's always better when Jack isn't here."

It is possible that she was innocent of Wilson's long association with Noël and of their great friendship, or that fatigue and the humidity had made her forgetful of it, but the remark was incautious, a lapse all the more surprising in a woman of great sensibility and kindness. Noël said nothing, and remained silent as we left the Y.M.C.A. to find Howard at the wheel of an open Cadillac.

"I'm sorry she said that," I managed to say before Noël spoke.

"Perhaps it's true," was the reply.

"They like to work things out for themselves. I think the two of them rehearse at night by themselves."

"Does Jack worry them, and stop things and start things all the time?"

"Sometimes. Generally he sits quietly and watches and gives them notes afterwards."

"It's the first time he's worked with actors of this persuasion, and it's the first time I've ever seen actors of this persuasion in rehearsal. It's quite new to me. In *her* case, very impressive. I don't much care how she goes about what she does, because she's a damn fine actress."

"She said the other day she didn't want to play for the results."

"For the what?"

"For the results."

"Whatever *they* may be. Did Jack know what she meant?"

"No, and he joked about it later, a couple of times."

"I want to talk to Jack about this. Perhaps a firmer hand is wanted, perhaps not. The important thing is that the *play* is being properly served. Do you think it is?"

"No. Not really."

"Why not?"

"The boy. The young man. He has a tremendous reputation and was wonderful in a play just last season, but he hasn't got the refinement or the fun for this part, and he'll never have it."

"No," Noël agreed. "Refinement is seriously lacking, and his speech is——what accent is that?"

"Indiana, Ohio—somewhere."

"There should be a certain affectation in his speech, the way those spoiled young men talk in life. That cannot be corrected overnight. However, when you are setting up for a New York production you'll find someone quite different."

It was the first inkling I had that there were plans for a New York production. It had been thought better that I not learn of the arrangements, and even my agent knew nothing of them. An acute shortage of vacant theatres was only one of the reasons that the plan never materialized. One of the great moguls of Broadway sealed its fate with the announcement—to Jack Wilson and the Theatre Guild—that it would never be seen in one of his theatres without the drawing power of a famous star in it, and, of the two or three who might conceivably have acted the mother's part very commendably, none was available for at least a year. Mr. Shubert also thought there was something snobbish in the play that he didn't like but could not pinpoint. A year later it won a cash prize from an eleemosynary foundation which financed the writing of a second play, yet *Within a Glass Bell* had a theatrical life of only eight performances at Westport the following week.

But before Mr. Shubert saw it, and saw Judith Anderson or Katharine Cornell in the role Miss Dunnock was playing, Noël tested my keenness in the ways of show business by suggesting that, fine as Miss Dunnock was, it might be wise to consider a First Lady of the Theatre in her part. It lent, he said, a greater excitement to the undertaking, and the character had been written with the kind of high theatricality one associated with a legendary star's performance. It was worth thinking about, he assured me.

It was too soon for me to assimilate this kind of wisdom: too soon, and I was too new at the game. I felt enormously privileged to have an actress of the caliber of Miss Dunnock speaking my lines and saw no other doing so, not by the most energetic stretch of my imagination.

On the way to a roadside place for a sandwich, we passed a tall man on foot, pencil-slim and dressed entirely in shiny black poplin, looking like a furled umbrella in the noonday glare. It was Basil Rathbone, who was appearing in Terence Rattigan's *The Winslow Boy* that week at the Country Playhouse.

"Extraordinary, isn't it?" Noël remarked. "How many people look like Basil Rathbone nowadays!"

There was more talk over club sandwiches and thoroughly refrigerated beer, and the greater part of it was about dramaturgy and in exactly what a good dramatic story consisted and how to tell at a glance that a dramatic premise was not a valid one.

"If the leading character has a *purpose,* an objective, a strong aim—take *Mister Roberts* as an example: all he wants to do is to be transferred to active duty—the other elements of the story and the other characters all dramatize the struggle to achieve that purpose. Every good play contains a question that is not fully answered until the final curtain. The question in *Mister Roberts* is simply: will he succeed in being transferred to active duty or won't he?"

I was applying this yardstick of dramatic validity to my play, trying to identify my characters' aims and place a definite interrogation point on the story that could be sustained throughout three acts. "My play," I said, "is only about preserving the status quo at all costs. Does that make it static?"

"No more so than *The Cherry Orchard* is static, and it's about exactly the same thing. The drama comes from external sources, threatening the status quo. The Russian man who says he owns some of the paintings, the young girl who wants to take the boy away, the message about the overdraft at the bank. What is missing only is the emphasis on these elements. The focus must always be sharp and definite, and some of Jack's staging is to blame.

"You notice how amusing your dialogue is?" he asked suddenly.

I nodded with a pleased smile.

"You didn't expect it, did you?" he asked.

"I hope it doesn't get big laughs."

"*Never* say that. A big laugh never harmed anything, unless it comes in the wrong place. The funniest line in all of Shakespeare is Hamlet's "Didst think I meant country matters?" and it comes just before the play-within-a-play, and I have heard it greeted with guffaws. I have also heard it go by unnoticed in a glacier of silence. Guffaws are better."

"I'd like to write a comedy."

"Yes, do. Immediately."

Later that day there was abundant evidence that he had managed to confer with Jack Wilson, for the first order of business at the afternoon rehearsal was to get Miss Dunnock up from her kneeling position in the second act at the point Noël had thought looked "old-fashioned" and to reposition her elsewhere and far more effectively. Other improvements were made in the staging, too, and I was asked to incorporate a few lines of dialogue here and there that made more emphatic the dire financial situation of the protagonists. It was my first experience of rewriting and came much more easily to me than I could have dared to hope.

Noël left for New York that afternoon in the open Cadillac, but his words stayed with me like an insistent melody that gets lodged in the brain and refuses to go away. There was a brief, firm handshake accompanied by an almost conspiratorial look: he seemed to be saying that he was relying on me to give Jack all the support it was within my power to give.

"And," he added from the back of the car, "don't, whatever you do, be nervous on the opening night. It's *such* a waste of time and spoils most of the fun."

I had had my first lesson from the Master.

3

The theatrical trade paper, *Variety,* reviewed the first night of *Within a Glass Bell* at Westport with such enthusiasm that the theatre box office was unable to satisfy the telephoned requests for tickets from interested parties in New York, yet at the week's end, when the setting was dismantled and the cast dispersed, I knew that no company of gifted actors would ever breathe life into the play again. Jack Wilson, having got his feet wet by directing something more substantial than the light entertainments for which he was well known, quickly undertook a new musical project to be derived from an old Ferenc Molnar comedy and, with expressed regrets, allowed his option on my play to lapse. I weathered the disappointment with a grace that surprised me more than it did anyone else.

Some months prior to the summer production I had been commissioned by Goddard Lieberson, then as now president of Columbia Records, to translate and adapt from the French one of Jean Anouilh's *pièces roses,* as their author designated them, a wistful, ruefully romantic play called *Leocadia.* The plan, which never materialized, was to provide a vehicle for Mrs. Lieberson, the actress-ballerina, Vera Zorina. The translation came easily; the matter of adaptation to the American theatrical climate was a problem never solved by me or by an English adapter when, five years later, the play reached the New York stage as *Time Remembered.* Anouilh's works survive a sea-change only very rarely, and their enchanting theatricality remains, for the most part, a joy to be experienced chiefly by French audiences. But the time spent in reshaping *Leocadia* sharpened a certain facility I had for comedy dialogue and increased my ambitions to write a comedy of my own. I wanted to construct a light and funny play that had in it something of the wayward sadness that Anouilh had managed to introduce into his *pièces roses.*

An idea for such a play came nearly tailor-made one evening when that splendid actress, Jean Dixon, told me at dinner about a liaison between a rich, married manufacturer and an unmarried lady of independent means that had been a true love story for more than two decades. The man divorced his wife finally and married his mistress, and the wedding breakfast was scarcely cold before their relationship disintegrated into open warfare. It seemed to me such good material for a comedy that I set to work on a first draft immediately, populating it with good parts, including one for a confused maidservant and another for a comedienne with a cynical view of life and a saucy vocabulary to match.

The basic confusion in it survived several drafts, that confusion being that the story was essentially a sad one and belonged to the genre of the French romantic theatre of the last century, whereas, in my treatment of it, it was gay and frivolous and touched only with the most delicate strokes of compassion and feeling. Yet it read well, had a number of really funny lines, and was optioned almost as soon as it came from the typist's. Herman Shumlin was convinced that the Lunts could be persuaded to appear in it, and a copy was dispatched to them at their Wisconsin farmhouse. Weeks passed before Mr. Lunt replied.

One night during this period of waiting I dined with the Liebersons and went backstage at the Majestic Theatre with them to be introduced to Mary Martin. *South Pacific* was still playing to capacity houses there, and going behind the scenes of a great big Broadway hit was a new experience for me. There was a delightful fragrance backstage, a potpourri of cosmetic odors and others resulting from hard work, dust, disinfectants, and a nameless smell that I could identify only years later as belonging to hemp and canvas. Miss Martin was radiant in her dressing room, displaying a new coat of pastel mink and inquiring if the color might not be too pale for her ginger hair; she seemed to care deeply for my opinion on the subject. Suddenly, appearing out of nowhere and clasping her in a bear hug, was Noël, chestnut brown from the Jamaica sun. Graham Payn, handsome as an advertisement for neckwear or cruises to the Caribbean, was with him. He had appeared with Miss Martin in Noël's musical, *Pacific 1860*, in London; had co-starred with Gertrude Lawrence in the revival of *Tonight at 8:30*; and had most recently earned superlatives in the English press for his singing and clowning in the Coward revue, *Ace of Clubs*. I had heard from Jack Wilson that he was Noël's favorite discovery and in some way, it was hoped, his heir to the kind of light comedy roles in musicals and plays that were Noël's exclusive property when he was younger. Certainly Graham had the presence of the true leading man and perhaps a matinee idol. With hair as shiny as wet coal, a winning smile and ruddy complexion, he brought something of the outdoors into the overheated dressing room. He kissed Miss Martin as if it were the fadeout of a particularly romantic film.

I experienced for what seemed an unconscionably long time a perverse anxiety that Noël would not remember me, although it had been no more than eight months since the Westport weekend; I turned away to examine bibelots and dressing-room ornaments, among them some of Miss Martin's collection of pairs of hands worked in metal and porcelain. The chatter was quick and amusing and sounded like operatic recitatives before the beginning of a beloved aria. Invitations to an impromptu supper were considered and declined; the next day was a matinee day. The health and vocal stamina of Gertrude Lawrence were discussed; she would play the first performance of *The King and I* a few nights later. The great world buzzed around me, exclusive to itself. Drinks were poured, and as I turned back to the group to accept mine, Noël winked and said, "How far along is the new play?" giving voice to something he could only have heard from the Lunts.

With that, with the tone of familiarity that established intimacy for all the rest to hear, together with the absence of a verbal greeting, the closed circle stretched its circumference to include me, and the joy I felt was nearly drunken. Miss Martin demanded to know what I had written and which play it was that would so soon be a reality, what was it called, please, and who was going to be in it? Without news from Wisconsin I could not say that the Lunts were thinking about it or anything other than that everything seemed to me to be all right. Noël grasped my wrist and squeezed hard.

"Just remember that hope springs eternal in the paternal heart," he said, with a solemn nod that suppressed laughter and made the remark sober and filled with concern. His words ratified a kind of agreement between us, one that had been totally unambiguous for me from the afternoon of our first meeting and continued throughout his lifetime. My own father was peevish and desultory, sometimes discouraging. I had found a surrogate *par excellence,* a parent of my adoption who encouraged me to go into his own business. I could not and must not disappoint him. I remember looking at his cufflinks, fashioned in gold to resemble ordinary shirt buttons, and thinking them a badge of such refinement I wondered that anyone could have had the wit to wear them or cause them, in the first place, to be made. I was confused with pleasure and I grinned.

In a moment the ugly reality of show business, there in the middle of the capital of success where every evening was enchanted, identified itself in dollars and cents. It was Miss Martin who asked if the financing for my play had been arranged for with certainty.

"It will be," said Noël. "Rest assured of that." The mink coat was resumed for his approval, and doubts about its color were renewed due to the variance in the way a vowel was pronounced. Miss Martin's English is accented with oval sounds of her birthplace in Texas, and "color" is softly pronounced in a way perfectly understandable to Americans but unclear to the English, who hear "collar" instead. Whether it was the shape of the shawl of fur around her neck that was in dispute or the tint of it took some time to unravel. Noël said he loved the "culler" of it and had never before seen anything its like, and Miss Martin said she worried over its fullness. Ah, well, perhaps she meant its "kahlah," thought Noël, in which case he found it very becoming and unusual. No, no, she meant the *shade* of the fur, because her hair was very nearly the color of the coat. The air cleared then, as did the eternal misunderstandings between the Americans and the English about the value to be given the letter "O," and the little gathering dispersed after kisses and handshakes all around.

"Of course," said Noël to me in a whisper on his way out, "she still says 'continue' as if it rhymed with 'when you.'"

He pulled his camel's hair coat over his shoulders and knotted a muffler at his throat. I longed to have been able to accept the general invitation to supper independently of the others. Perhaps I would have done had I known it would be four and a half years before I saw him again.

4

The Lunts did not appear in my comedy, though in refusing it they expressed their admiration for the writing in a way that went beyond the ordinary needs of courtesy, and Herman Shumlin did not produce *To Be Continued.* It was put on at the Booth Theatre the following spring by Guthrie McClintic, who directed it in a mixture of styles that merely stressed its already blurred focus, with a cast of fine actors that included Dorothy Stickney and Grace Kelly. After reading the newspaper reviews the morning following the opening night, I suppose I might have been expected to shrink from public view; instead, I went to Sardi's for lunch and talked about the new play I was writing. Disappointment and failure toughen one up for battles to come, and I went back to my typewriter with renewed determination and some fresh technical equipment for the craft of comedy. The Lunts had gone to London to appear in Coward's *Quadrille,* an enormous success which he had written specifically for them and promised to keep them occupied for a long time, and I trained my sights on someone else for whom to manufacture a vehicle.

Finally, in the autumn of 1955, I had a success on my hands. *The Desk Set* was no great shakes as a play, but the witty performance of Shirley Booth, for whom I had written it as if I were stitching her into a becoming dress, raised it above the level of commercial claptrap in the audiences' minds and spread good cheer among everyone except the critics for two seasons. It was an assured success before its tryout performance in Wilmington, Delaware; the film rights had been sold to Hollywood for a handsome sum before the curtain went up. At Westport, in talking about great theatrical personalities, Noël had said that a good practice for young writers to follow was to study the individual comedy techniques of a given actor or actress, to observe him (or her) playing the same role over and over again, noting the various tricks he employed, the subtle variations in speed or emphasis he used with different audiences, in an attempt to discover in what precisely his magic lay. It helped considerably, he said, when one set about writing a role for a star, to have studied that star thoroughly. With Miss Booth I had done just that, subjecting her to almost surgical analysis before writing the character she was to play. The results were happy: as a glove-maker I had taken careful measure of her hand.

Noël took Edna Ferber to the New York premiere, and we met again in Miss Booth's dressing room after the performance, where, it seemed, the entire audience was gathered to congratulate her. It was so noisy that anything beyond the briefest exchange was unintelligible. Miss Ferber limited herself to two words: "Very funny." Noël kept nodding his head rapidly with half-closed eyes. He had something he wanted to say but wasn't about to shout it. I pushed my way through the barrier of people trying to pay their respects to the star and was finally near enough to Noël so that I could hear him. He bent forward a little in a conspiratorial way, squeezed my arm, and said in a sibilant whisper, "I see you have followed my advice."

That was all, and nothing more was needed. I felt sure he would be at Sardi's later with all the first-nighters, loud with drink and chatter until the morning newspapers arrived with the critics' reviews, but he wasn't. I had planned to invite him to a quiet lunch somewhere one day that week. A day or so later I learned he had left for his house in Jamaica, where he planned to spend the winter working on a new play.

That winter I received permission from the directors of the Actors' Studio to attend their "sessions" every Tuesday and Friday morning and observe in silence, without participating in the discussions that followed, the experimental work that was being done there. The Studio then enjoyed the esteem of being the fountainhead from which all theatrical greatness flowed, in America, at least—an eminence that was quite disproportionate to the actual contribution it made to the show business community.

Located in a disused church in New York's Hell's Kitchen, the Studio was the American tabernacle of the Stanislavsky "method" which had for its bible the writings of Konstantine Stanislavsky, a codified set of principles instructing an actor in how he might best prepare to undertake a given role. These dicta, originally put into practice at the Moscow Art Theatre, had for their vicar and interpreter the American director Lee Strasberg, one of the Studio's founders. My twice-weekly visits began as pilgrimages to see the "scenes-in-progress" performed and hear them discussed, but my interest soon waned with the repetitiousness of the lectures Mr. Strasberg gave at the end of the sessions, and my visits became less frequent. The following autumn I stopped going altogether. A young actress I knew reproached me for my loss of faith. "I don't understand you," she said; "even Noël Coward goes now!" I could scarcely believe my ears. I thought he was in London preparing the production of *South Sea Bubble,* but a few telephone calls established that he was making one of his infrequent visits to New York and that one of his reasons was to observe the classes at the Studio. When I reached him by telephone we arranged to meet for a drink after a concert he was going to at Carnegie Hall.

The rendezvous was arranged for a pleasant little saloon on West 45th Street. The Theatre Bar was a mecca for eager young actors in search of employment as well as those already gainfully at work in the Broadway area. Drinks were poured in good measure and at a price much lower than in similar establishments nearby; the traditional sawdust was on the floor and the place smelled of hamburgers and beer, but Noël nodded his approval of the environment the minute he set foot in it. We had not been seated more than a few minutes before the long, narrow room was buzzing with the news that Noël Coward was present; it was as if a high-tension wire had just been identified as threatening the customers' safety. The young men and women gathered there were, for the most part, members of the "methodist" cult; if not actually accredited communicants at the Studio itself, they were at least the students of those who were and paying handsomely for their instruction. Noël, for them, represented the enemy, the proponent of stylish acting and beautiful speech, meticulous timing and rigid discipline of performance. They seemed to be breathing contaminated air in his presence, yet stared at this rare and curious bird as if he were something in a zoo. He sensed the hostility immediately and enjoyed it thoroughly.

Among the gathering were two young men I knew slightly as drinking companions, both actors not working at their profession that year, both students of an acting teacher who was a good friend of mine, both argumentatively dedicated to the dogma of Stanislavsky. One worked as a part-time taxi driver when not engaged in classroom acting and rehearsing; the other worked thirteen weeks each year in summer stock and survived the winter on unemployment benefits and casual odd jobs. Their efforts to get my attention or at least to acknowledge their presence were nearly comic in their extravagance, and Noël suggested that I invite them to join us for a drink. Chairs were pulled up, introductions performed, and steins of beer ordered. The taxi driver undid the zipper of his leather jacket, folded his arms as if he were about to pronounce sentence on the guilty, and asked, "What did you think of the Actors' Studio, Mr. Coward?"

The question should never have been asked, really. The poor innocent had no idea that the box he was opening contained so many things.

"I've been several times, you know," said Noël.

"Do you like it?"

"Tell me your name again. *Henry?* Henry, I am absolutely *fascinated* by it."

He signaled for another scotch and began very slowly.

"The place is chilly and uncomfortable, but I didn't mind that, having rehearsed and directed behind more old clocks in dusty drill rooms of the Territorial Army than any retired sergeant-major, but the chill came from the gathering and not from any hole in that deconsecrated roof. They gave off the distinct feeling that an enemy had invaded their camp. Not unlike here and now."

Both young men shifted somewhat uneasily in their chairs.

"I represented to these people in their untidy clothing a useless remnant of the past, a Punchinello past his prime, and one who had never had anything to offer beyond the most capricious of entertainments. Then, too, a reputation for snootiness has accrued to me, which anyone who knows me at all would contradict at once. I have known cabmen with a greater hauteur than I should ever dream of attempting to assume."

The cabman unfolded his arms and tried to look less haughty and aggressive.

"However, one must take into account the spectacle I presented to them, seated there dressed much as I am now and resembling more than ever a heavily doped Chinese illusionist, which is how I always describe myself. But I regard myself as less of an anachronism there than the young millionairess in her paint-stained dungarees and soiled tennis shoes."

Henry mentioned a name as famous as Rockefeller, and Noel nodded.

"What did you see them do, Mr. Coward?" asked the other one, called Will.

"The park bench scene from *Liliom* is very à la mode there now. They play it and replay it, if one can call it that, to a fare-thee-well, these people—a man and a girl who might conceivably be thought ideal for the parts by the directress of some amateur theatrical group on an especially underpopulated desert island.

"To say that their style of acting is 'hesitant' would be to accuse it of being too forthright and speedy. Had I not known *Liliom* quite well I should never have thought that it was a play of Molnar's they were attempting."

Henry and Will tried to identify which actors he meant, but Noël shook his head in ignorance of their names. "The man appeared as one of the longshoremen in *On the Waterfront*, I believe. The scene in the original is not very long, no more than ten minutes I should say, if that, but as presented the other morning it endured for at least three-quarters of an hour."

Will tried to explain that it was a classroom, not a theatre.

"Oh, yes, I was mindful of that all the while. By no wild exercise of the imagination could it be said to be directed towards the comprehension of an audience, one that had paid money for its seats. When it was done with, the man and the girl breathed deeply several times, rather showily, and then Mr. Strasberg asked them what they were working for, to which the answer quite clearly could not be 'the money.' Well, the girl had an odd answer for this. She said she was in search of an identity. Her interpretation, she says, of the play is that Liliom appeals to Julie because he is in search of an identity as well. I have thought and thought about where this dubious aim is suggested in Molnar's text, but I fail to see it. There is a good deal of jargon they use that I don't understand, but the girl referred to 'using' her own emotions from the times in her life when she was troubled with self-doubt. She said she spent the greater part of the morning beforehand staring into her bathroom mirror and asking herself who she was, and it became gradually clear that the identity she was seeking was her own and the self-respect she was trying to arrive at was *hers* and not the character of Julie's. This seemed to me at once like such a total misunderstanding of how to prepare a scene that I waited for Strasberg to interrupt her, and he finally did. But what he spoke of then bore no relation whatever to anything he had just seen or anything the girl had said. He embarked on a kind of—shall I say tuneless?—aria, punctuated by wheezes, about the nature of acting, reminding himself of the excellence of two Italian immortals he had seen in his youth, namely, Salvini and Duse."

"Did you ever see Duse, Mr. Coward?" Henry asked.

"Several times when I was very young, but I didn't understand Italian at the time. Now Strasberg tried, without any facility for narrative or any descriptive power, to convey what it had been like to see Duse on the stage. He dwelt particularly on her hands and how memorably she moved them, and the girl hung upon his every word—you should have seen it—as she made the effort to apply Duse's hands to her own identity crisis. I really did feel for her. Have some more beer."

It was, I think, principally the supremely charming way he talked to them that disarmed them of all argumentative power. Years later, when I first heard Noël called "The Master," I was to remember his lecture to the young actors and how they attended it as if sitting at the feet of a sage. It was evident in their faces that they were listening to more than the voice of experience; they were hearing wisdom, and knew it, and would argue it back and forth between themselves and repeat it to others like them for a long time to come. That it was also impeccably spoken and so rapidly synthesized by his intelligence was a matter for their astonishment, too. Will looked about himself from time to time to see if the others in the saloon appreciated the excellence of the company he was in and to measure the degree of their envy. Henry really wanted to hear what Duse was like.

"I think," said Noël, "possibly what one remembers best of her after all these years is her voice. Her voice was precisely like a stringed instrument that one imagined to have fallen into disuse when the viola came along to replace it. That is the only comparison I can think of. I can hear it perfectly in my memory's ear whenever I wish to summon it to mind, because it was unique. Absolutely *unique*. And, appropriately, the voice spoke Italian, with that language's rich, long, dying syllables, so that everything she said was inherently musical.

"And next, one recalls the timing. I never saw Duse in comedy, but I'm willing to bet she was a superb comedienne. Of course, tragic acting is far, far easier than comedy acting; they differ in their approach as night differs from day. Actors who are equally at home in both styles are very rare, but Duse was surely one of them. Because, in the tragic roles she played in London, she timed every movement, even of her eyes, as if she were counting by some mysterious numerical system known only to herself, and that is the technique of comedy applied to the problems of acting in a tragedy.

"There was one little play she did—a sort of curtain-raiser— which belongs to that genre of unadulterated claptrap that only very great actresses indeed seem to know how to find. I believe there once was a shop somewhere on the Continent that sold these curtain-raisers in lots, but it has evidently discontinued its custom. Bernhardt had a trunkful of them. Duse was able to transform the arrant nonsense of this one-act vehicle into the kind of thing that legends are made of.

"At one point, I remember, she sat on a kind of stool, one elbow on a table beside her, twisting a lock of hair that fell over one ear. She sat silent for a time, quite a long time, as she was able to communicate a series of quite contradictory thoughts without saying a word. She had a difficult decision to make, as they always seem to have in Italian plays, and was weighing over every possibility in her mind, you see, and she was able to make every one of these different possibilities perfectly clear to us in the audience, one by one. What she did was to accompany each change of thought with a savage little pull at the lock of hair. I saw her do this

little play at least four times during one brief season in London—
I think it was the spring of 1921—and this action, the tweaking of
that lock of hair, never varied for so much as a split-second from
performance to performance.

"Now that is consummate artistry, achieved only by the exercise of a superior intellect confronted by an unusually difficult
acting problem. I don't mean that Duse was a brainy woman,
though the kind of companions she kept round her suggests that
she was able to hold her own in elevated conversation, but it was
her cool, controlled intelligence, untroubled by nerves or uncertainty, that created this really extraordinary effect of making us
read her thoughts. And the effect was created entirely by deep
concentration and tugging at her hair at *unvarying* intervals.

"*That* is technique.

"I longed to be permitted to take the floor from Mr. Strasberg
that morning and say there exactly what I have just said, but a
natural timorousness in my nature survives from childhood. I sincerely believe Mr. Strasberg to be essentially a very kind and
thoughtful and certainly idealistic man, but a man with great difficulties of articulation. He tries to say what he means as best he can
to people who are evidently far less perceptive than he and quite
obviously lack his education and scholarship."

I had planned for the evening to be of quite a different character from the way it was turning out. It was perhaps the only chance
I would have of seeing him before he hurried back to London for
the rehearsals of *South Sea Bubble,* and there were things I wanted
to discuss with him privately. I had been struggling with a new play
that was in danger of dictating its own shape, and I felt uncertain
of my control of the difficult material; I was still too diffident to ask
him to read it, but I had planned to talk to him about it anyway.
Further, I worried that I had led him into a social trap and that his

behavior was dictated only by his excellent manners. But he appeared to be enjoying himself thoroughly, lecturing Will and Henry about Duse, and as he went on about Lee Strasberg he had the air of a man committed to setting things right in the minds of the young. Nowadays, recalling him, people who knew him only slightly invariably speak of Noël's "kindness" to them, as if he had been the last person in the world they expected to exhibit more than the normal, everyday courtesies and were astonished in some way by the intensity of the interest he took in them and what they were doing. I was myself astonished at the concentrated way in which he persisted with his discourse and feared that it was really falling on deaf ears, that he was preaching to the unconvertible. Yet each movement I made to suggest that the hour was growing late and that it was time to go was met with a small, silencing gesture. He was not to be sidetracked even for a moment.

"What Mr. Strasberg meant to say to the assembly of fledgling actors, among whom I recognized a few highly paid professionals, was that Duse was a genius, with which anyone who ever saw her would readily concur. I don't think he was attempting to *define* genius—I don't think anyone would be so rash as that. But he was *describing* genius in acting and the methods genius employs, and was ascribing to Duse something he had no way of knowing about and that I believe to be totally wrong—he suggested that she was able to project any number of deep feelings and make her audiences share them with her by the sheer strength of her ability to experience these emotions at the same time she was planning to do so, as directed by the text or her understanding of it.

"Now that is nonsense, and dangerous news for those who, however gifted they may be, lack years and years of experience before the public. Very great acting is something entirely different, and a careful reading of Stanislavsky merely confirms it. Very great acting is the imitation of the outward appearances of emotions that were experienced at an earlier time, and privately, one hopes.

"For an actor to achieve this, as Duse and a few others have done, requires the exercise of the intellect in selecting and simplifying the choices of what one means to do long before one ever faces an audience with them. It is easy to talk glibly about this, but it wants the most diligent care and watchfulness, with one ear attuned to the stopwatch and the other to the audience.

"I am both emotionally and intellectually unable to understand how *feeling* anything at all while giving a performance can be any help—unless it be the feeling that the audience is very slow to react, or too quick to laugh, which is terribly unsettling in comedy and has been known to spoil many an actor's carefully prepared performance.

"Sublime actress that Marie Tempest was, she could never understand what Duse had meant to say when she tried to pay Marie a compliment, and Marie used to repeat it as if it were some kind of joke. Whereas it seemed to me to be perfectly clear, simple and wise. Duse had said that acting was dancing, one, two, three. Anyone who has ever watched a ballet rehearsal can understand exactly what Duse was talking about. But poor Marie thought she meant something was lacking in her own physical grace and allure on stage, and puzzled over it for years."

"Who was that? Who did she tell that to?" Henry asked.

"Dame Marie Tempest," I said, stressing the first word.

"One of the most sublime actresses I was ever privileged to see and to work with," Noël explained. "She could pour out a cup of tea onstage and send a comedy line winging right up to the back of the balcony without the slightest apparent effort and make it sound as if she had just invented it."

Will and Henry exchanged glances of wonderment. Will in

particular, a talkative and even garrulous fellow by nature, appeared to be at a loss for words. He had given up seeking the admiration of the other customers and waited breathlessly for Noël to say more. Noël sipped his scotch. Henry voiced his worst fear.

"You don't like American acting at all, Mr. Coward?"

"I regard many American actors as being in many respects superior to our own in England. Marlon Brando, for one, despite his having told me that I wrote plays as if I didn't know that there were people in this world who are starving to death. I'm told he's a millionaire now. I wish I were."

If any ice remained congealed then, it melted all at once with that remark. Henry roared and Will beamed, and Noël said, "Where's the bloody loo?"

While he was away from the table Will said he would like to buy Noël a drink. I had some knowledge of the state of Will's exchequer and said it wasn't necessary and certainly wasn't expected, but Will insisted, and the table was furnished with another round. When Noël returned, he inquired what they were doing and what their prospects for the future were. Henry said he drove a cab. It was parked nearby, and when Noël was ready to go home he would be happy to drive him.

"Only if the meter is turned on," said Noël. "You're not disdainful enough to drive a cab."

"I'm working on it," said Henry. "It's an acting problem."

"Perhaps you can explain something to me," Noël said. "What does Mr. Strasberg mean when he talks about an effective memory? Or an *affective* one?"

The roles were reversed, deftly switched by Noël so that now Henry could deliver himself of opinions and judgments born of his experiences with his own teacher, a man of infinite patience and imagination who, although a disciple of Strasberg, had a great respect and liking for the more traditional acting techniques as displayed by the English. An amiable mood informed the rest of the evening, and Noël laughed heartily from time to time, showing no particular signs of fatigue with the others. He ordered another round of drinks. Their relaxation was so complete that Will's and Henry's vocabulary began to be seasoned with all the impolite words they knew, but Noël raised his finger in a gesture that called for an attentive silence.

"You don't need to use those words, you know," he said. "I generally just say 'Zsa Zsa Gabor.' It means all those things."

There was some more technical talk then, about how Charles Hawtrey, the London actor-manager in whose company Noël had appeared as a boy and who, he said, "taught me everything I know," had taught him to raise his voice by a half tone every time he turned upstage so that his words would not be muffled or lost upon the audience. He said he wished the young actors in New York would devote their time to a study of vocal projection and clear speech instead of to the investigation of their psyches, and urged Henry and Will to work on scenes from Shakespeare with this end in mind. Then it was time to go, and Henry fetched his cab to the entrance of the saloon. Will said good night and Noël agreed with him that it had indeed been a very pleasant evening. Noël and I settled into the back of the medallion cab.

"He hasn't thrown the meter," said Noël.

"He's off duty," I said.

We deposited Noël at the doorway of the building on East 54th Street where he maintained a small apartment, and Henry had one more question to ask him before he could permit the evening to come to an end.

"Mr. Coward, I get the impression you think the Actors' Studio is a bad thing."

"No, no. Let them have their little games."

"I'm trying to get an audition for them so I can be a member. Would you advise me *not* to?"

"Henry, you must know what's best for yourself. But as I said to my friend Maureen Stapleton, who is a superlative actress, when I saw her at the Studio the other morning, 'What on earth are *you* doing here?' She looked embarrassed and said, 'Well, Noël, you know, it keeps me off the streets.' And I said, 'You *should* be on the streets!' " He turned then with a little wave and disappeared into the building.

On the way back to the West Side, where I was living, Henry remained silent. He seemed troubled, and sighed heavily.

"What's the matter, Henry? What are you thinking about?"

"I'm thinking: what a wonderful, wonderful man."

5

A chance to discuss with Noël the play I was writing never materialized. He flew off to London for the rehearsals of *South Sea Bubble* sooner than he had planned and did not visit New York again until the following spring, when he spent only a few days negotiating for a New York production of his comedy *Nude with Violin*. We saw each other here and there, at large gatherings where it was impossible to exchange more than a few pleasantries; a tentative engagement to meet for an hour for an after-theatre drink had to be canceled, and when I telephoned him at his little apartment on East 54th street it was invariably Graham Payn I spoke to. He would explain the demands on Noël's time and deplore them in a weary voice that expressed wistful longings to be quietly away in Jamaica, where he and Noël shared a house.

The Desk Set was then touring the Western part of the United States, playing lengthy engagements in San Francisco and Los Angeles and later Chicago, and I used the tour as an excuse to distract myself from the troublesome business of the play I was writing and rewriting with a firm conviction that it was going to be very fine and that it would be shown to no one until I was entirely satisfied with it. There was something to be learned, I told myself, from seeing The Desk Set performed before provincial audiences and measuring their responses against those of audiences on Broadway. What I learned, if anything, was that theatregoers are very much the same wherever one goes. They are present in the theatre for one simple reason: they wish to be entertained, a fact that Noël insisted on all his life and repeated regularly when he was confronted with high-minded, abstruse offerings that pleased no one. It is not a bit of wisdom, though, that can be learned secondhand, and it can only be assimilated slowly. It is all the more difficult to accept when the serious drama you are writing is giving you trouble. Noël's view was that even the works of Sophocles could be regarded as entertainment if they were exceptionally well done, although they would necessarily appeal to a much more limited audience than, say, a knockabout farce. What he objected to mostly was the pretentious and the sham, the political tracts disguised as great drama and the experimental plays undertaken by accomplished writers in other fields who lacked theatrical expertise. There was no subject under the sun, he held, that could not serve as a valid basis for a good play, provided it engaged the audience fully and entertained them and, not incidentally, made them line up at the box office to buy tickets.

I had, in those days, the box office very much in mind. A number of quite respectable serious plays by established dramatists had failed to find favor with Broadway audiences, even though their critical reception had been excellent. The play I was writing, *Faster! Faster!,* was filled with anger and vituperation, and at least two of the four major characters were argumentative and disagreeable. I foresaw a good deal of resistance to some of the unpleasant observations about American life that I made in it, resistance from audiences and possibly from producers before the audiences ever had a chance of seeing it. I tore up the first two drafts and started fresh. I found that some of the anger expressed in the earlier versions was my own, directed at the characters I was writing, and not their anger with each other. I sweetened the temper of the play with funny lines and a lighter, more considered touch. I put it aside for six months and tried to forget everything about it so that when I read it again I might look at it with a greater objectivity. The six months passed as a prolonged holiday of late nights and partygoing and a daytime idleness that produced only vexation and a vague sense of time seriously wasted.

But when I read the play again I was delighted with it. My agent was so impressed with it that she put it up to the highest bidder among five Broadway producers. The result was that I was doubly enriched, by the contractual arrangement for its production and by meeting for the first time the producer-director who signed the contract, Carmen Capalbo, a witty and cultivated man who has remained a good friend even though the play never reached the stage. Carmen and I were lunching together at the Quo Vadis restaurant one day in the autumn of 1958, celebrating the motion picture sale of *Faster! Faster!* to Warner Brothers and the signing of a contract to write three movies for them. There was an exceptionally good bottle of Mouton Rothschild with the rich Italian food, and a Havana cigar with the espresso and brandy, and together we must have created the impression that we spent the middle of every day of our lives in this kind of languorous festivity, although I rarely ate more than a sandwich for lunch and never drank until dinnertime. At least that is the impression I feel sure that Noël took away with him after he had crossed the restaurant, where he was lunching with a lady I didn't know, to greet us and chat briefly about his own play and then mine. *Nude with Violin* was entering rehearsals the following Monday, and mine had just been postponed until the following spring to accommodate the schedule of an actress Carmen and I hoped would agree to do it. Spirits were very high. Our laughter was a shade too loud. I remember thinking that Noël frowned slightly before asking me to telephone him and wondered if it manifested disapproval. When I did manage to reach him at his apartment later in the day, there was certainly only jolly good will in his tone, and we agreed to meet later in the week for lunch at Sardi's.

When we met, the day was unseasonably warm and the restaurant overheated. Noël mopped at his brow with a patterned handkerchief and expressed the Englishman's perpetual bewilderment at the temperature of American interiors without saying a word.

A large wooden bowl of salad was set down on a serving table near ours and he craned his neck to peer into it, glancing back at me with his lips pursed in distaste. "I *abhor* iceberg lettuce! It is indigenous only to this country, and I don't think it is grown in any recognized agricultural way. I think it is manufactured for them. Yet it garnishes every plate everywhere you go. And here they offer up more of it than is usual. They once gave me a lot of it under some fresh pineapple. Ersatz stuff!"

Valentine, the maître d'hôtel, took the order, but not before the health of his family was inquired after and news solicited of an elderly waiter who had retired that year. "Val," he said, indicating the salad bowl at his right, "I want a very large plate of that delicious iceberg lettuce in which you specialize here, and I want it garnished with a very rare filet mignon." Valentine winked with understanding and an ambiguous smile. I had thought of ordering a chef's salad, but asked for cold roast beef instead.

"You're very fond of food, of course? Yes, so are most writers, but some of them make a fetish out of it, planning and discussing what they are going to be eating three or four days hence.

"Some years ago I sat next to a famous American lady writer at a dinner party in London. We had been put side by side because it was said that she was eager to know me. The food in this particular household is customarily remarkable, course after course of postage-stamp-size portions, all sublime. The woman fully appreciated the excellence of the fare, devouring every crumb with almost exaggerated relish. But she didn't talk at all, even during the pauses between courses. I finally gave up trying to start a conversation and simply chatted with the lady on my left. Not until the dessert course appeared did the lady novelist say a word. She touched my arm and said in a very important voice, 'There is nothing that can quite touch the English strawberry.'

"Maugham, you know, has a habit of planning his travels gastronomically. If Alan Searle proposes that they stay three days at the Gritti in Venice, Maugham is likely to say that two is enough. One day for the *risotto con pesce* at Burano and the second for the scampi at Harry's Bar. What he has in mind for dinner I don't know. Perhaps they eat at the hotel. If you mention some out-of-the-way place in France, Maugham searches his memory, which is no longer trustworthy at his great age, and comes up nodding with the name of some dish that is characteristic of the region."

I invoked Ian Fleming's name as one of the writers who could not stop talking about food. "Yes," said Noël, "and you go to his house in Jamaica and receive the most awful culinary shock of your lifetime. Expectations understandably run high, with all of those wonderful meals eaten throughout the Bond books. They're enough to make one reach for a chocolate to sustain one. And then he serves you an unripe avocado, an undercooked mullet that smells of the laboratory, and a coconut-and-egg pudding that appears to be exhausted from the effort of making it. Meanwhile, as you are trying to look like an appreciative guest, he tells you how precisely to kill an inkfish. I'm not going there again."

I asked if there was an equivalent to Sardi's in London, a good restaurant that catered especially to the theatrical world. He named one, and his description of it was so exact that when I entered it for the first time not long after, I had an overwhelming sense of having been there before. "One is surrounded by lipstick-red satin everywhere and one feels one is dining in a whore's coffin. But the food is exceptionally good."

Valentine was answering the telephone at the other side of the room when the filet mignon arrived at the table and turned out to be exactly what Noël had ordered; the meat was the center of a huge lettuce bouquet. He asked the waiter to bring him a large empty plate and, when it arrived, removed the lettuce leaves one by one with his fingers and arranged them neatly on the second plate with a touch that suggested he would have preferred to be wearing gloves. Then he summoned a busboy. "Take all of that away," he said, "and present it with my compliments to some vegetarian, or other needy person."

He tucked into the beef then with relish and inquired after the tenderness of mine, making a cross of his knife and fork on his plate and pausing before leveling a loaded question at me. "Do you have those giddy, costly lunches at Quo Vadis every day?"

"It was the first time I've been there," I said. "I generally don't eat lunch. But Carmen thought we should celebrate selling the play to the movies, and also a three-picture deal I just signed."

He nodded with approval and addressed himself to the beef, interposing brief, direct questions between bites. "Who is going to be in the play?"

"We need two big names, possibly three. And the best policy nowadays is to go after Hollywood names, provided they have stage experience or came from Broadway originally." I identified three or four major film personalities with whom tentative conversations had already been held, and specified the one I considered an ideal choice for the leading woman.

"Dear boy, you must be extremely cautious about choosing film actors. No matter how good they may have been originally as New York actors before they became movie stars, the totally disorganized process of filmmaking has changed them in ways not even they suspect, and very often their temperaments are such that they have forgotten how to give a sustained performance. You must tread very, very lightly. And tell Mr. Capalbo I said so."

I said I would. I named several instances of Hollywood stars having returned to the Broadway stage after many years' absence and having given fine performances.

"That is no doubt true, but I can counter with just as many names of those who were merely embarrassing. Wouldn't it be better to cast the play entirely with fine New York actors whom one knows to be reliable?"

"The theatre shortage is now so acute that you can't get the Barrymore or the Plymouth or one of the good playhouses unless there is a star name to pile up a healthy advance at the box office. So we are *obliged* to think the way we're doing. We've already had to postpone because all the theatres are booked solid until next March."

"Yes, not long ago I was forced to take on a disastrous leading lady because it was believed she would be a huge attraction, and I don't think I have ever regretted anything so much, in a career of a not inconsiderable length. But you probably know all about that."

The actress he was talking about is not a great favorite of mine, but there is no cause to be ungallant, and certain details which might identify her as surely as a fingerprint, such as the name of the play and the season that included it, have been omitted here. Noël himself did not name her, except in a whisper when he had finished describing what it had been like to direct her, and his reasons for spelling it all out in such detail were motivated not by vindictiveness but by the wish to put me on my guard against similar professional entanglements with stars of unproven ability. He left a bit of his filet on the plate and settled back into the banquette.

"We were in rehearsal only a few days before I realized that what I was dealing with was essentially an amateur. She had, of course, the enchanting voice she has used to advantage before, and she was almost pretty, but there was absolutely nothing in her equipment that anyone with a modicum of sense would call technique. I saw at once that I was going to have to give acting lessons.

"Her estimate of herself and her importance to the world of the theatre was unparalleled in my memory, as I never met Sarah Bernhardt, and so it was an extremely delicate matter to suggest that our evenings after the rehearsals should be spent together, going over her part minutely. She was amazingly quick to copy to perfection whatever I demonstrated for her to do. Her split-second timing was an absolute revelation to me until I came to understand that the timing was identical to my own and that everything she did was splendid mimicry.

"She might, of course, have got away with this in the theatre, with no one the wiser, had she been able to reproduce more than once any given action or way of delivering a line. She was totally incapable of doing anything more than twice. Having got it right, she would immediately do it again in the identical fashion and stop and look at me for my beaming approval, which I was quick to give, and when it was time for her to do it once more, she would come up with something entirely new and every bit as awful, on the whole, as what she had been doing earlier and that I was attempting to correct.

"This total inconsistency of performance was a great trial to the other actors, all capable farceurs, who were unable to arrive at a conclusive way of playing a scene because of her habit of never being in the same place twice. An actor with his back to her, for instance, would wheel about in his place to point an accusing finger at her and deliver his line, only to discover that she had wandered away from her mark and was toying idly with some ornament ten feet away. One by one they came to me begging to be allowed to quit, and one by one I seduced them into staying; in one instance, with an unnecessarily extravagant offering from Cartier.

"There were the usual arguments about dresses and wigs, of course, and in this regard she behaved exactly like the very great star she mistakenly imagined herself to be, even taking a pair of shears to the hem of a garment designed by one of the two or three greatest dressmakers in the world. I had already thrown up my hands in despair and steeled myself for the disaster that was to come, when she came to me in tears and said that she simply could not continue to play with a company of inferior actors and hoped that the production could be interrupted and recast completely from a list of actors she had already prepared.

"I am not often speechless, but on this occasion I stammered incomprehensibly.

"I no longer remember the exact words, but I was merciless with her, stopping just short of using the word 'amateur.' I do recall her saying she was willing to wager a week's salary that I had never spoken to Gertie Lawrence that way, and I was so shocked to hear my darling Gertie's name appear in even the remotest connection with this wretch that I saw red. But somehow the waters were calmed, and we struggled through to the opening night.

"It was dismal, of course, and the actors hurried their lines so as to get to the final curtain as rapidly as possible and be done with the whole ghastly business, except for my leading lady, who contrived to play throughout the evening at a pace more suitable to Chekhov than to farce. This contrast of speeds served her well, in that a kind of brainless charm was the effect of her slowness, and she would pause as if deciding what to say next, filling out the pauses with little clearings of her throat, which was understood by many to be witty comedy technique but which I knew to be nerves."

Sardi's excellent coffee was poured and Noël lit a cigarette. "Well, you saw it and read the notices, so you know how *I* came off, my reputation once more re-examined and once more found to be quite unjustified by Mr. Atkinson and Mr. Kerr, but the bitch emerged as the darling of the town, didn't she? She was applauded so vigorously when she walked in here on opening night, you would have thought Mrs. Fiske had come back to life."

He lowered his voice to a more confidential level lest someone overhear. "[She] is impersonating someone, and I'm convinced the American public knows full well that she is, and is waiting to find out *whom*. And the minute they do, of course, her career will be terminated. I should love some chocolate."

Valentine suggested an ice cream dessert with a meringue and bitter chocolate topping and Noël said he didn't mean that: he wanted *candy,* possibly Brazil nuts or nougat in a thick dark-brown wrapper, but it was not an item on Sardi's bill of fare. "Chocolates help my music considerably and my piano keys not at all," he mused.

We talked of friends we had in common, of films and plays we had seen. He had visited Boston for the opening of a new musical in which he had no personal interest other than curiosity and had gone to Philadelphia to see a play a friend of his had written and another friend, John Gielgud, was directing. This latter he thought was of the highest merit and very original, but he worried that it would not find a ready audience in New York. "I made myself useful there. I gave out a few notes."

It is a common practice for dramatists and directors to see the productions of their friends in the tryout cities or the summer theatres and to offer counsel or make specific suggestions for improvements in the writing and staging, as Noël had done with me at our first meeting in Westport, but to give out "notes" to actors is properly only the business of the director of the individual production. I thought it sounded like an impertinence for him to be making suggestions to actors when they had John Gielgud as their director, but I restricted myself to saying that I was surprised Noël was handing out "notes" in Philadelphia.

"Oh, nowadays I hand them out right and left."

The remark came back to me many years later with the resonance of a bell clanging in the memory when Elizabeth Wilson, a fine actress and comedienne who had appeared in my only successful venture on Broadway, was reminiscing about the play in Philadelphia that Noël had seen.

"One night Noël Coward gave me a note. Can you imagine?

I wasn't happy with what I was doing, particularly in the early scenes, and I kept doing too much, or something. I think I was being too emphatic right after my first entrance.

"One night after the performance," she remembers, "I was taking off my makeup and feeling depressed about the whole thing and making horrid faces at myself in the mirror when there came a little tap on the dressing-room door. My heart jumped into my mouth when it was Noël Coward who came in. I had never actually met him, and naturally I was in complete awe of him, and there he was, having climbed up all those flights of stairs to see *me,* standing there and introducing himself, as if *he* needed an introduction! He sat down and gave me a very searching look and said he had a *note* for me, and I was so thrilled I think I giggled.

" 'You are a very brilliant actress,' he said right away, 'but you are doing something quite wrong, a tiny thing at the very beginning, and it damages everything you do later on.'

"He quoted one of my lines from the first scene—and, by the way, every word of it was right—and told me that by saying it the way I was saying it, positively and slowly and making a big thing out of it, I was robbing my character of any growth and any element of surprise for later on in the play. He suggested treating the first scene very lightly, throwing it away in an offhand manner. He advised me to do the rest of the play exactly as I was doing it, and see if then the whole thing wouldn't fall into place for me neatly and comfortably. I didn't understand what he meant at all, but I thanked him profusely and he said good night. And he must have told John Gielgud the same thing, because the next day at rehearsal I had the same note from John.

"Well, I thought, anything was worth trying, and I did it the way he told me to, never understanding why, and it worked. It changed everything. It changed my whole performance. I could feel it from the audience and from the other actors, that now I was doing it *right*. And all it was, really, was a matter of throwing it away as if you didn't care about it. Can you imagine? How did he *know* that? But he knew it, and wanted *me* to know it, and climbed up all those stairs to tell me so!''

Elizabeth's memory came as no surprise to me: I was already familiar with that side of Noël's nature that had prompted his visit to her dressing room. I had heard dozens of similar stories in London as well as in New York.

But that day at Sardi's it seemed to me to be a discourteous violation of the director's prerogative to give a note without his permission, and I said so.

''Oh, I don't mean that I am actually *epistolary*, but I do consider that more than four decades' experience as an actor counts for *something*, and that there are actors here and there who might benefit from a little of it. Even as a boy I often told my elders that they could do something in a better way, and I suppose it was cheeky of me, but more often than not I was right. The Lunts do it all the time, always have done. The minute they see an opportunity for improvement, they are right there with their notes. They do it to each other from breakfast onwards. Acting with the Lunts is nothing more nor less than one long note-giving session, which is why they are the superb actors they are. They polish and refine every little nuance until it is perfection itself, and still they are not satisfied.

''Have I never told you the famous story of Lynnie and the handbag? I shall never forget it. Let's have more coffee.''

The restaurant was nearly empty, and the tables around us were being laid for the evening meal. Noël seemed to be free of appointments for the rest of the afternoon; there had been some talk of a movie with Joan Crawford he wanted to see, but I much preferred to hear about Lynn Fontanne.

"When we all appeared together in *Design for Living* many years ago, I remember one afternoon following a Saturday matinee Lynnie coming to my dressing room in the Music Box Theatre in New York in a state of great excitement.

" 'I've just had the most marvelous idea,' she said, 'for the last act.' She had always said that the character she was playing was the kind of woman who had a messy handbag, all stuffed up with the totally unnecessary things women are always carrying about with them. She had seen a woman in a restaurant at lunch that day whose purse was so crammed that its contents rose like a soufflé when she opened it, and she wanted to do exactly that in the last act.

"I said I thought it was a brilliant idea and asked at what point she would like to do it. At one point we were seated together on a sofa, and I rose to cross to the other side of the stage with my back to her. It was then that she wanted to open her bag, sure it would get a good laugh, and she didn't want me to be puzzled or confused if I heard a laugh where there hadn't been one before.

"She planned to introduce the bit of business at that evening's performance and was hurrying over to some little man on Eighth Avenue who would fix up a kind of watch-spring arrangement in the bottom of the purse. Then she would cram it with all kinds of old silk stockings and notebooks and things, and of course she would rehearse it and time it until she knew she had it right, but she wanted me to know about it in advance so that when the laugh came I wouldn't suppose that something had gone all wrong.

" 'Do you mean to go to all that trouble,' I asked, 'knowing that this evening's performance of *Design for Living* is our very last together? That the engagement ends tonight?'

" 'What possible difference would that make?' she replied, giving me a fishy look, and swept out of my dressing room with a faint air of superiority."

Two women had been lingering over their luncheon coffee at a table across from us some twenty feet away and I had glanced at them from time to time, aware that their own conversation had come to a halt and that they were quite shamelessly eavesdropping on ours. Noël spoke quietly, but his voice carried as easily across an empty restaurant as it did a theatre filled to capacity. When they rose to leave, one of them, a sweet-faced matron with a gardenia pinned to the lapel of her suit, came to where we were seated with pen and paper in hand.

"Oh, Mr. Coward," she gushed, "Juné says I shouldn't bother you, but I simply *must* have your autograph."

"Of course you must; no one should be without one," he said kindly, signing the slip of paper and dismissing her by turning sharply to me and trying to remember what we were talking about.

When the woman had gone, I asked him if it wasn't a chore being recognized everywhere he went.

"Much better than *not* being recognized, let me tell you, although that too has its amusing possibilities. I tried to send an opening-night telegram over here at the Western Union office on Broadway long ago, when La Guardia was the mayor. I signed his name to it, the wire being one of my jokey ones. But the clerk said, 'You can't sign Mayor La Guardia's name to this!' I asked why not. 'Because you aren't Mayor La Guardia!' So I scratched out his name and wrote in my own. The woman looked at me and said, 'And you can't sign Noël Coward, either!' 'But,' I said, 'I *am* Noël Coward.' 'Oh,' said she, 'in that case you can sign Mayor La Guardia.' "

He checked his watch for the time. Discovering that we were too late for the start of the Joan Crawford movie, he suggested that I have a brandy with my coffee. I hesitated, then agreed to have one, planning to drink it very slowly, that the pleasure of his company might be prolonged.

"It *is* very hard to get away from it all *entirely*," he said. "Although I do my best. I have my retreats. Jamaica is best. Very few people come to stay. At Montreux the situation is different. We're invariably there throughout December, and my birthday comes along then with all its attendant brouhaha, and Christmas, which I dearly love, and Joan Sutherland is a neighbor, and the house is always full of David Niven and others, but still I very rarely emerge from my private rooms before dusk, if I'm working, which I usually am.

"I couldn't, I don't think, be completely alone. There must always be someone there. Someone you know so intimately you can sit for hours with, without having to say anything. That is real peace, I think, and real friendship. But if I'm acting, of course, the situation is so different. It is almost impossible to get away. You cannot run off to Lorenz Hart's famous small hotel in Bucks County on a Saturday night in November and come back to New York Monday afternoon completely refreshed. There will always be somebody in the hideaway hotel to say, 'Oh, Mr. Coward, you must come and see my windmill and have lunch in it,' or something equally imperative. And then the word spreads like a yawn that you are in the vicinity, and the next thing you learn is that Beatrice Lillie is nearby as well. And that, of course, is the end of that.

"I am not surprised to see New Yorkers rush away on Friday afternoons even in the dead of winter, but where they go seems to me equally populous and awful. Have you never been to Fire Island?"

"Yes. I hate it."

He toyed with a cellophane wrapper he had removed from a cigarette packet. "It may have been all right, once, when it was a gangsters' hideout. But now it is really fearful. I was promised something totally different. I went once to stay with a friend. We went to some kind of shack on the beach for a steak, and my presence there caused such vibrations of excitement that scarcely a plate was touched as everyone stared. This woman a moment ago reminded me. A woman who seemed to be made entirely of leather came up to the table and asked if I was Noël Coward, and I said yes, I was. 'I thought so,' she said. So I said, 'Yes, I *saw* you thinking it.'

"Next morning there was a continuous stream of people whose gait seemed to slow down very perceptibly when they passed the house where I was staying, obviously trying to get a glimpse of me or, better still, say hello and get my autograph. So I fled to the dunes with the *Times* of London crossword puzzle, and there wasn't a soul visible for miles, but within minutes there was a great, hairy man in a canvas cap staring at me from a few feet away. I recognized him as having been with the woman in the restaurant the night before.

" 'How do you like Fire Island, Mr. Coward?' he asked. I said I had never been there. This caused him to laugh uneasily. 'Where do you think you are now?' he wanted to know. So I said 'Deauville,' imploring him not to tell me that it *wasn't* Deauville, as I had come such a long way to see it. He withdrew in confusion then, but soon the woman appeared, looking more like a dragon than she had the night before, wearing a sort of great cape of plastic. She stood quite near me like a sentinel and would probably have remained there until sunset except that I looked up from my crossword and asked if she happened to know a nineteen-letter word meaning 'very,' at which point she told me that if I didn't know *that,* then I wasn't Noël Coward and marched smartly away. It went on like that all weekend.

"Are you going to that party Saturday night?" he interrupted himself.

Years later, recalling similar afternoons of desultory conversation with Noël, over coffee cups, brandy snifters and starched table linen, when his monologues were self-interrupted by an amusing anecdote that was nearly always pertinent to the main body of his argument without appearing to insist too much on its specific application to me, I recognized his uncanny ability to synthesize. He had an elliptical approach to his "lessons." He began them as if he had, in reality, nothing of any importance to say. He amused, he delighted, he engaged the attention. He introduced "asides" that made me laugh loud and hard, a laughter that I knew to be inappropriate to the surroundings. When I blushed, as I always do when I laugh heartily, he would shoot me a look that suggested he feared for my health, or my sanity, or both.

That day at Sardi's he introduced a theme he would return to again and again throughout the next decade. I call it his "urbanity" lecture. He employed the word in one of its older senses: the state of being "citified." Whenever we were together thereafter, this topic was never entirely missing from his talk. He had an insidious way of interpolating a mild reproach to me in the presence of others that must surely have puzzled them, as members of the same family will refer darkly to some ancient matter or classic disagreement between them in a way that excludes their companions and makes them briefly uncomfortable. These reproaches were like those of a father who is thoroughly resigned to the fact that his son is a prodigal whose disobedience is a personal affront. If I swallowed a yawn at the luncheon table, it would very likely produce a sharp look and a few words: "Jean's party went on till very late, did it?" or "I forgot, you don't get up for lunch."

There was a trap in his question that day that I could not have anticipated. I said I was looking forward to the party very much; after-theatre suppers in pleasant surroundings in the company of people I liked and admired afforded me great pleasure. He rubbed his upper lip thoughtfully as if it itched him. "You really ought to go away somewhere. I cannot *think* why you stick to this city as you do. It's stultifying and quite horrible, really. Yes, if one is actively engaged in production and you have something in rehearsal, it is essential to be here, and then the city takes on a meaning and becomes stimulating in itself.

"Do you stay up late every night as you used to?"

"Well, you know I'm a night person; yes, I stay up late."

" 'Night person' is what Fowler would call a 'vogue term,' and like all such terms it should be avoided. It suggests you aren't yourself by day."

"I'm not. My metabolism is such that I think better at night. I definitely work better then. Sometimes I go home after dinner and sit down at the typewriter and work straight through till three or four in the morning."

"It's just a bad habit you've got into." He shook his head. "Set the alarm on your metabolism to coincide with the sunrise."

"If I ever see the sunrise, it's on my way home from a party."

"Probably a rowdy one," he cut in, almost unkindly. "I strongly recommend that you get out of here, away somewhere, to an entirely different environment, preferably one where the two greatest events of the day are the sunrise and the sunset, and where the people are simple, kind and uncultivated. People who have never even heard of Broadway or Shaftesbury Avenue are the best."

I made excuses then, none of them any good. He continued to shake his head slightly.

"I take it you've read my autobiography, the first volume, *Present Indicative?* Somewhere in it you will find a paragraph that begins with the phrase, 'Between the years 1917 and 1919 I knew . . .' followed by a list of names of the celebrated and some of the damned all in one lump. What it meant was that I was progressing like wildfire before I reached my majority.

"Now, dear boy, when you are very young, as I was, and before you have become completely unspoiled by your success, the only way to assure that this horrid putrefaction of having enough money in the bank and your likeness appearing in every Sunday supplement does not seize you and cause you to be shunned èverywhere is to study carefully the outward signs of how others weather the tragedy of success. I was fortunate in this regard and, being an observant young man, was able to learn very rapidly what to do and what not to do.

"One did not, for instance, quote from newspapers the praise one had learned by heart, nor even refer to the fact there was a photograph in that week's *London Illustrated News* which one's listener might not have seen, and, bite one's tongue though one must, one did not even obliquely refer to a royalty check for a truly magnificent amount that had arrived in that morning's post. Nor, if you were wise, did you go out and spend a large portion of that royalty check on the outward appearances of affluence, such as cigarette cases from Garrard's in imitation of Michael Arlen."

"I know that. I made a few mistakes at first, naturally. Most people do, don't they? When you suddenly have enough money for the first time in your life, you go out and buy things and give expensive presents to people who have been kind and generous when you were struggling."

"Don't interrupt. With people who have already arrived, I found, one had to walk on eggs, being neither too subservient nor too familiar with them. I remember when Miss Janis told me to call her 'Elsie' I was very pleased and full of myself. A few years later, when I was saying, 'Please call me Noël,' I knew that everything was all right."

"I always called you Mr. Coward," I said, "until you told me not to."

"And quite right you were. But do follow what I am saying. One of the things I learned at this time was not to get drunk. In fact, I drank very little in the company of my peers and betters. Arnold Bennett thought I only drank water."

I swirled the brandy in my glass with a little smile that was meant to say I believed it had been offered to me as a kind of test.

"When *Cavalcade* was launched, it was a louder success than I had ever dreamed it would be. I was presented to the Royal Family in their box at a special gala and a few days later took off for South America on a very slow boat indeed and proceeded to take stock of myself."

"I read that in *Present Indicative,*" I said.

"I never lacked for fine company, and I adored all the trappings of the rich, full life, but there was a severe ache somewhere between my ears whenever I was exposed to too much of everything, the people and the Napoleon brandy and the Aubusson carpets and the Renoirs and all that. Worldly, amusing and gifted people always have a way of making demands on my time and energies that—if I allowed them to—would stifle me and be merely the prefaces to renewed claims for attention. If I have a sincere regret, it is the waste of time spent in amusing people simply because I was expected to do so.

"This is not to say that I don't do it well, or enjoy it while I am doing it. But it creates a very distinct tension in me, and I have often thought I would be far better off quietly at home contemplating my navel or admiring the shadow of my profile on the wall."

"That is a different Noël Coward you are talking about."

"A much nicer one, too." He flashed a little smile, as if to say that I was seeing something of that other, more private, *persona* at the moment. "Long ago, in a song called 'Weary of It All,' I referred to 'caviar and grouse in an overheated house,' and I think that about says it, don't you?"

I argued a little then, very gently. The play I was readying for production the following spring had for one of its principal characters a woman of the *grand monde* Noël was referring to with such disdain. I had used a number of real-life characters to form a kind of amalgam in the writing of her, an embodiment of elegant unhappiness copied directly from models in Santa Barbara, Southampton and Park Avenue. I said that without firsthand knowledge of how these women behaved, looked and spoke, I should never have been able to write her as I had done, and that, certainly, moving in exalted circles was a necessary part of a writer's life.

"Not nearly so necessary as moving in circles at the opposite extreme. Shall we go?"

We moved towards the entrance then, but our departure was interrupted by the young Italian bartender, who had some new snapshots of his infant son he wanted Noël to see.

"This is Vincente?" Noël asked. He nodded in admiration of the plump child and studied the snapshot for a time, as if there might be something to learn from it.

"So fortunate, isn't it, that he resembles your wife?"

The bartender laughed in agreement as Noël gave him one of his winks. Then we were out on West 44th Street again, grimacing against the Indian summer.

6

The party we were both bidden to the following Saturday night, on the topmost floor of a residential hotel in the East 60's, was catered by the nearby Colony restaurant; there was neither caviar nor grouse and the penthouse was not overheated. The fare was that of the classic New York after-theatre party: baked Virginia ham, white meat of turkey, a cold vegetable salad in mayonnaise garnished with lettuce that Noël must have acknowledged as not having come from a factory. A couple of black waiters in striped livery circulated unobtrusively with trays of drinks. It was organized smoothly in every detail; the host's expertise at such matters was well known and guests rarely disappointed him with tele-

phoned regrets at the last minute or the news that someone uninvited would be coming in their company.

It was not a party to "meet" Noël Coward, so far as I remember. Most of the people there appeared to know him well, if not
intimately, and were on easy terms with him. Some of them had
known him before I was born. Ten or a dozen of them might have
been grouped in that anonymous galaxy he had identified at the
restaurant a few days earlier as those who made excessive demands on his energies, and possibly he could foresee what would
be the order of the evening, for when he entered the large living
room, with its several sofas and long couches, he elected to sit in
a good light at the very center of the room.

By placing himself there and chatting amiably with a distinguished New York attorney who joined him almost immediately
and sat down at his side on a diminutive sofa that would not
accomodate three persons comfortably, Noël established ground
rules for the field of action as distinctly as if a games master had
pronounced them; the other guests stayed close to the periphery
of the room, perching on window sills when all the chairs were
occupied, as if some centrifugal force had engineered their placement. From there they might come forward and greet him, singly
or in pairs, chat briefly and enjoy a laugh, but they would not
remain for very long. There was always someone else jockeying for
position, to nudge them aside and displace them. Noël was, in his
way, giving an audience, and the room became a theatre-in-the-
round. One expected something to be enacted in the center, and
as only life knows how to imitate art, an impromptu entertainment
developed soon after Noël arrived. Laurence Harvey had only
quite recently come to the public's attention as Romeo in a lackluster film of Shakespeare's tragedy, had married Margaret Leighton,
and crossed the Atlantic to star with Julie Harris in Wycherley's

The Country Wife on Broadway; his performance as a fop in this play was somewhat too extravagant for American tastes. He portrayed the foppishness offstage as well, and in an era when dark silk lounge suits, white shirts and subdued neckwear were the uniform for well-dressed men about New York at night, Harvey appeared at the party wearing heather tweeds, a mauve shirt that matched his lisle socks, and a magenta tie.

He crossed the room conspicuously to greet Noël, interrupting his conversation with the lawyer, and boomed, "Noël! I had no idea you were in New York!"

Noël looked up at him without a sign of recognition. "Who is it?" he asked.

"It's *Larry,* Noël."

In English theatrical circles, the diminutive "Larry" is the exclusive property of one man, the man who is now Lord Olivier; it has remained so for at least three decades.

"You seem to me to have changed drastically, Larry," said Noël, and turned back to resume his conversation, but Harvey plumped himself down between the two men, and the lawyer shrank back into a corner of the sofa to make room.

"Larry *Harvey,* you dear man," he said. "I *must* talk to you about something."

"I see," said Noël in a stricken voice, and talk was exactly what Harvey did. For at least an hour that seemed three times that length to everyone else, the discourse continued in a vocal monotone that set the speaker distinctly apart from other members of the English acting fraternity with its emphatic flatness and unvarying volume. The subject was Harvey, and nobody seemed better equipped than Harvey himself to enlarge upon it; there were his performances in regional theatres and repertory companies to be recalled and described, his theories of what Shakespeare had meant to say in certain speeches from the lesser comedies, his plans for his own *Macbeth,* his own *Richard II,* his own Hotspur. "Have you never longed to play a particular part in Shakespeare, Noël?"

"I've always thought I'd be particularly good in *Romeo,"* said Noël, "as the Nurse."

It was his single reply to Harvey: the rest was monologue that allowed of no interruption. I stood in a corner where I could hear all of it and glance from time to time at Harvey's wife, who had come to the party later than he and found an old friend she hadn't seen in many years; they remained in the vestibule chatting away like schoolgirls. Margaret Leighton was, then as now, a very fine actress with a cool blonde beauty and the authentic air of a gentle-woman that is seldom found among the pedigreed community of today. Her models belonged to a different time as, I think, Noël's models for being a "gentleman" were the well-known companions of the heir to the British throne when the century was young.

Maggie Leighton was not only Noël's friend and sometime co-star, she was indisputably a member of the English theatrical Establishment. A half dozen of these eminent artists were then appearing in New York (Miss Leighton was acting in Terence Rattigan's twin bill, *Separate Tables*) and being lionized at just such parties as the one being given that night. That her husband was foolish and long-winded and sartorially out of order was an uncomfortable reality for Noël, but it was one he was prepared to deal with in the only way that seemed to be within the bounds of good taste for all concerned. The occasion called for a "gentleman" who could suffer a fool gladly, and the only thing for him to do was to listen attentively and assume his "Mahatma manner," an aspect that combined wisdom and forbearance and neatly disguised the impulse to rush off headlong into the night. Glasses were replenished again and again; the assembled company fell nearly silent in attendance on the scene; what conversation there was limited itself to the lowest tones, even whispers, so that as the supper was laid out in the next room the sound of cutlery against porcelain was as loud and jarring as in a noisy restaurant. I stood in my corner, apart from the others, nursing my drink and enjoying the scene as if it were the second act of a drawing-room comedy. Mrs. William Rhinelander Stewart, an enduring ornament of the New York social scene, fingered her pearls and inclined her head in a way that summoned me to her side.

"For God's sake, go and rescue Noël from that outrageous man!" she hissed.

"I think Noël is handling it beautifully," I said, and we stood watching together as Harvey began to perspire and dried the palms of his hands on a lilac handkerchief. Noel's repertory of attentive nods appeared to be limitless; his focus was centered exclusively on Harvey's face and often directed to the movement of his lips, as if by reading them he was better able to understand what was being said. Once or twice he cupped a hand about his ear in the manner of those who are partially deaf, as though he could not endure to miss a word.

On and on it went, the words coming in a compulsive rush, like some diabolical mechanism that cannot be switched off: the "other" Larry and the great Edith and the one and only John were summoned, along with other Olympians of the profession, to augment the star turn and, in their absence, called only by their Christian names. Hollywood was denigrated in a familiar way and those obliged to work there pitied. Noël swallowed a yawn.

If the scene thus enacted had been carefully written as a morality play, it could not better have dramatized Noël's point at Sardi's three days earlier: that very little was to be achieved in gatherings such as these and much to be lost, that diversion meant precisely what the dictionary says it does—a turning aside from a course of action; and, moreover, that the time wasted in such company was a valid basis for regret that endured long afterwards. With this in mind I wondered, in fact, why he had elected to come to the party at all. Only later I learned that the host was to be the principal investor in *Nude with Violin* and that he could not, in all conscience, have gracefully declined to appear. But "appear" was the exact verb for his presence there. Harvey did all the talking, but the star was Noël Coward, placed center-stage for all to see, suave, impeccable, suffering a fool like a gentleman and yet totally in command of each moment.

Mrs. Stewart yawned. I yawned. The contagion spread. "For the love of God, Larry," someone said from a corner, "you've got the whole room yawning like caverns."

The company was redistributed then; a plate of food was brought to Noël; someone spilled a drink. Harvey dispensed charm and news of his plans to those who had arrived too late to have overheard them earlier. Noël set down his plate and rose to come over for a chat with Mrs. Stewart and me. The endurance contest with Harvey wasn't mentioned. Soon he said it was time to go home, set down an unfinished drink and bowed lightly to one and all with a valedictory smile. The host came over to show him out.

"Will you call me, Noël?" Harvey shouted from a far corner.

"I certainly will," said Noël, and kissed Janet Stewart on the cheek, adding under his breath, *"many* things."

He said hello and good night to Mrs. Harvey in the vestibule, where an admiring group had collected about her. Harvey went to the buffet table to examine it, dabbing at his brow with his livid handkerchief, clearly aware that he had just played a scene that had not lived up to his expectations. He toyed with some turkey and stuffing on a plate, set it down on a window sill, poured himself a large whiskey and looked about for a sympathetic ear. "I've been talking such a lot, I'm hoarse!" he said, to anyone who would listen.

Noël had permitted Laurence Harvey to embarrass himself mightily without once having contradicted him or introduced an argumentative note into the hour-long stream of self-advertisement, and Harvey had known what was happening and yet had been unable to stop. No one had told him to go on, or encouraged him, or supported him in his need to identify himself as a newcomer who would make the English theatrical world sit back and acknowledge him as a genius. To have silenced him with a quip would have been easy for Noël, but also unthinkable. Laurence Harvey was the husband-of-the-moment of Margaret Leighton, friend and peer. The English theatrical Establishment must preserve its face in New York. Noël had had, in fact, no other choice.

His treatment of Harvey, once he had gone, made me laugh. Years later, when I mentioned the incident to him, Noël had difficulty in recalling it. "Why do you remember it?" he asked.

"I thought it was the most extraordinary thing I'd ever seen, the way you just let him go on and on and on. And, in a way, the most *gentlemanly* thing, too."

He reflected a moment. "A good way to deal with arrogance," he said, "is simply to allow it to exhaust itself."

7

A few months later *Nude with Violin* was happily settled in the Belasco Theatre, and Broadway audiences had an opportunity of seeing what had been absent from the American stage for nearly two decades, the consummate comic artistry of Noël Coward in conjunction with a company of superlative actors with whom he had often played before. There was a sense of occasion about every performance he gave and the audiences rose to it handsomely. I have rarely heard such uniformly happy crowds in the American theatre, and a new generation of enthusiasts was exposed to the glossy fun that their elders remembered fondly but feared had long since vanished from the stage. The Stanislavsky method adherents were pleased, but puzzled. Some of them went back to see it several times, like spies invading an enemy camp. It was easy to dismiss the play, a nonsensical confection about a fraudulent modern artist who had died and left his multilingual butler to sort out his confused affairs, but the high level of Noël's comedic skill could not be disregarded by those who had never witnessed anything like it before. Mr. Strasberg graciously urged the communicants at the Actors' Studio to study what Noël was doing, which they dutifully did, and they talked all winter long about what they had seen without ever betraying the slightest understanding of the technique that had gone into the performance.

During the three months' limited engagement, it was possible to observe a side of Noël I had heard about—a side he had stressed in the two volumes of his autobiography—but had never had a chance of confirming for myself. Much has been written about the discipline the theatre exacts from those who are dedicated to it, and much of it is mere cant, but nearly everyone who has published views on the regimen of the performer is agreed that a great deal of rest and quiet is essential if an actor is to sustain a role for eight performances each week. Lynn Fontanne has repeatedly described her own method and urged others to do likewise: she simply stayed in bed until late afternoon and spoke only when it was absolutely essential to do so. Even so much as an apéritif before her pre-theatre supper was forbidden, and while she would eat a hearty meal after the performance and have a few drinks and gossip with friends until well after midnight, such outings were proscribed on the nights before matinee days and kept very brief on matinee days themselves.

Noël was not quite so rigid as Miss Fontanne, being of a sturdier nature, perhaps, but he adhered to a strict regimen all the same. He slept long hours, avoided talking on the telephone by day, and idled away the afternoons at the piano. He frequently went to the movies. The social whirl of New York caught him up only rarely, and when it did the occasion fell on a weekend. Never fond of exercise, he kept his figure trim with a high-protein diet and limited his intake of alcohol to a few scotch-and-sodas after the theatre. The city's well-known hostesses were heard to complain that he was totally inaccessible. "No one in this world needs *that* much rest," said a particularly ambitious one, and her rivals would have been quick to agree.

I saw very little of him that winter—during which time the production of my play was once more postponed until the following autumn—except for an occasional cup of tea in the afternoon or a chance midnight encounter at Sardi's which never failed to produce the remark, "Don't stay up all night." I had begun to make plans for a protracted visit to Europe and read a lot of nineteenth-century works that involved the Grand Tour. Sandwiched between these excursions to a Continent that no longer existed, I read a Coward short story that somehow had escaped my attention. Reading it at the time was especially appropriate, following as it did upon Noël's advice to me to put myself at a remove from New York and to avoid the company of the fashionable darlings with whom I was spending so much time.

His story took its title from Keats's "Ode on a Grecian Urn": "What Mad Pursuit?" ("What struggle to escape?"). Its matter was simply that of a man who desperately needed two days of uninterrupted rest before embarking on an arduous lecture tour throughout America and who agreed to visit a country house for a weekend in the promised certainty that there he would find that rest. Reading it, I was struck instantly by the parallel circumstances of the moment, with Noël turning down invitations right and left and keeping to himself as much as possible. The story was one of social embarrassment and horror that Noël had turned into a kind of agonizing comedy of bad manners that is nearly unique in modern literature. A great deal of it was, so to speak, written between the lines, and long-ago celebrities kept peering out from behind their masks of fiction to demand recognition. Not even the most fertile of imaginations could have fashioned it out of whole cloth. I wondered what the circumstances were that had produced it, and asked my friend Mrs. Stewart, whose memory for social irregularities is reliable, what she knew about it. She remembered it as having been written many years before after a house party at the Doubledays', but said she couldn't be sure, and suggested I get Noël to tell me.

When I saw him in the privacy of his little apartment on East 54th Street one afternoon that winter, in the sitting room that seemed to have yielded almost all of its floor space to a Steinway baby grand, we drank tea and munched biscuits, and Noël Coward the raconteur held forth without interruption on the story behind the story of "What Mad Pursuit?" He needed no more than the slightest cue to embark on the whole wretched history, for it was evident that he had regaled many people with it before and that it had become polished and refined in the telling to the point where he had made accommodations for the inevitable interruptions of laughter, with little pauses and nods of the head as if he were performing on the lecture circuit. Though I have set down this monologue as faithfully as it is possible to render it in Noël's words, several figures must still remain anonymous, which is curiously appropriate, as in the story there is frequent repetition of a modish phrase of the period, "who shall be nameless"; this innocent jest followed immediately upon the specific identification of somebody.

The circumstances were these: One frigid night in February,

1937, Noël found himself huddled under a fur lap robe in the back seat of a Packard limousine that was as capacious as a train compartment. The car was en route from the middle of Manhattan to a house in the distant Hamptons, where he was to stay until the following Monday; both house and car belonged to Cobina Wright, a social luminary of the thirties whose parties attracted every bit as much attention then as those given by Elsa Maxwell, having the added cachet of being backed by her own considerable fortune rather than that of somebody else.

She was giving one of her smaller parties in the back of the car. A fine stock of beverages was at hand: an open bottle of Taittinger in an ice bucket, a thermos container of black coffee laced with brandy, old bourbon and older scotch; there were wafer-thin sandwiches of *foie gras* to sustain them until they reached their destination, where a proper supper was waiting. With only six hands between them (Clifton Webb, in earmuffs and a camel's hair beret, was the car's other occupant), the preparation of drinks offered certain problems. Owing to a failure of the illumination in the back seat it was pitch dark and not always easy for one hand to know what the other was doing, so Mrs. Wright hit upon the idea of a running commentary to ensure that the right drink wound up in the right hand.

"Clifton is now pouring scotch into your glass, Noël, which I am holding in my left hand, and you are holding my champagne in your left hand and my cigarette in your right, which you will put into my right hand as I give you the scotch from my left when Clifton is finished pouring it. Then I will set down the champagne glass on the floor and pick up the brandy bottle as Clifton hands me his glass for a refill."

It was the beginning of what had been foreseen as a "quiet" weekend. Noël was then playing eight performances a week in his anthology of nine one-act plays, *Tonight at 8:30,* performed in repertory with Gertrude Lawrence. He played three very different parts nightly in three separate programs, and in three of the plays he was obliged to sing and dance. To get out of town following the Saturday night performance and spend the time until Monday afternoon in seclusion at somebody's country house was the only thing that sustained him, and Cobina Wright's offer of such a haven, where he didn't even need to appear at meals, had seemed ideal.

"She promised me," Noël said, "that Clifton would go to sleep the minute he reached her house and not be heard from until Monday when it was time for him to go back to town. He was said to be as exhausted as I was from the rigors of whatever play he was in at the time, but he exhibited no signs of it in the car. He started out by being amusing about somebody's divorce and then tiresome about his mother's new furs. I dozed off for a time, but whenever Clifton needed another drink, Cobina would wake me up to hold her glass in one hand and her cigarette in the other while she told me what I was doing as if addressing some especially retarded child."

The chauffeur was doing his best not to skid on the glacierlike roads and stopping every few miles or so to scrape frost from the windshield; ten miles per hour was its average speed once the car was in open country. "All in all," said Noël, "the journey seemed longer than the one on the Trans-Siberian railway, though without the amusing frontier stations."

On reaching the Wright house, Noël declined to help himself to any of the supper savories keeping hot in réchauffé dishes, and yawned so elaborately that Cobina showed him directly to the room he had been assigned.

"It looked as if Lady Mendl had made a few incautious suggestions, which were followed to the letter," he recalled, "and it was overheated, and the bathroom had a communicating door to the room Clifton would occupy.

"Exactly what this meant became instantly clear when Clifton appeared at my bedside in embroidered pajamas and announced that he was going to read aloud from a slim volume of verse he had written. It was five in the morning, but he switched on all the lights and began by telling an unpleasant story about Cole Porter and another about Marie of Rumania, both of whom had failed to assist him in some charity function and were therefore the objects of his free-floating scorn. Everyone knew that her poor, dear Majesty was a screaming nymphomaniac, but that she was quite sane on most other subjects, and I think Clifton might have forgiven her this one excess.

"I fell asleep during the reading of the verse, which was free in form and very Chinese, and woke in the morning with all the lights still on, when a maid came in with my breakfast tray and the news that a blizzard was in progress. My body ached unmercifully and my head felt as if it had been stuffed with hot cotton wool. The maid said that we were entirely cut off from the outside world, and I looked out over the gardens, which were like an arctic wasteland stretching blissfully to infinity. Irrationally, I bathed and dressed, when I ought to have crawled right back into bed, but I had some vague plan of going to sleep again directly after lunch and having my dinner sent up to me on a tray. And anyway I could hear Clifton snoring away behind that connecting door in the exact rhythm of the 'Hallelujah Chorus,' which would have made sleep impossible. So I explored the house, which was enormous, and found a long, enclosed verandah offering a restful view and deep porch chairs with high backs. I settled into one of these and was about to doze off again when some movement outside caught my attention.

"A long caravan of Rolls-Royces and Pierce-Arrows was approaching at a snail's pace in the distance, like a funeral cortège for some eminent gangster, except minus the flowers. I sat glumly watching the limousines disgorge their passengers in the driving snow and wondering why so many of the cars had California license plates. I also remember thinking that it would make an admirable subject for Cecil Beaton's camera, all that black against white.

"Cobina's voice kept echoing through all those vast rooms, screaming my name, as the house filled with people, and it dawned on me that I had been invited as the star attraction for a huge lunch party and that I would be expected to resume my public personality for the benefit of her guests."

A sixty-foot heated swimming pool had been installed in the cellar of the Wright house, and when Noël was captured finally by his hostess and led belowstairs to say hello to "the few friends who just happened to drop by," he saw that Grace Moore was spectacularly present, that Carole Lombard had brought her streaming head cold with her, and that a contingent of film cowboys whose names were then household words was already splashing about in the steaming water. Slightly more conventional professions were represented by the scions of at least two major publishing dynasties, along with their mothers-in-law, stepchildren and dachshunds, and a titled Englishwoman who was a Governor's Lady in some remote colony of the Crown.

"There was an ambitious luncheon arranged on a buffet table at one end of the pool, which was as hot as bouillabaisse, and the assembled company was already showing signs of having taken alcoholic refreshment. I was handed a black jersey tank suit and told to get into it in the changing room, and I took a drink in there with me and sat down gloomily on a wooden bench. Presently one of the movie cowboys whom I had seen again and again on the screen but had never met came in dripping wet and greeted me as if we had been at school together. He said he was completely misunderstood in Hollywood, where there were no longer any gentlemen left, and that one had to choose one's company there very carefully indeed.

"I said, somewhat ambiguously, that I thought that was true practically everywhere, and he seized me by the shoulder and told me that I was the only person in the world who could rescue him from the mediocrity of the movies, and didn't I think he would cut a fine figure on the London stage? It seemed to me that if the precise extent of his theatrical ambitions was to cut a fine figure, I might safely agree with him, and did so. Whereupon he gave me a sort of bear hug and spilled a good deal of his drink on me. I thought it would be best after all if I got into the swimming suit, and he left me alone while I did so.

"I was partially undressed when one of the other movie cowboys came in and, seeing me with my trousers off, made a most explicit sexual advance. I turned this into a joke by giving one of my artificial laughs and saying that he was a foolish boy.

"At the poolside Grace Moore was lying flat on her back and singing 'Mi chiamano Mimi' from La Bohème, and the mother of America's most distinguished publisher plied me with liverwurst and Spanish onion and told me that a great friend of mine had been selected to play Scarlett O'Hara but that Mr. Selznick had sworn her to secrecy. As Vivien Leigh was not even thought of for the part until many months later, I wonder to this day whom she meant.

"Then she brought her grandson over to meet me, saying that he was a prodigy, and left us together. He was no more than fourteen years old and very pink all over, and he wanted to know exactly how much I had been offered for the film rights to the plays

in *Tonight at 8:30,* saying that he knew Metro-Goldwyn-Mayer
was interested, but not very much, and that they were only really
looking for a vehicle for Norma Shearer.

"He lectured me on the iniquities of agents, and then lowered
his voice to tell me about his collection of pornography, which did
not compare to his father's but was coming along nicely. He asked
me, not entirely irrelevantly, if I was a friend of Jean Cocteau's, and
when I said I was, he said all he wanted in this world was a letter
in French from Cocteau with some dirty drawings in the margins.

"Then he directed my attention to a pretty girl of about thirteen, the stepdaughter of a different and rival publisher, who was
so drunk that two very mannish ladies with unshaven legs were
supporting her in her passage to the ladies' changing room, where
she was later heard to be very sick.

"The boy told me the mannish ladies would be having a fight
soon, and minutes later one of them accused the other of having
made an indecent suggestion to the drunken child, and the other
countered with the accusation that the first had been flirting with
Grace Moore's chauffeur and that Grace was very angry about it.

"I looked about helplessly for some means of escape and
found it only when an overweight lady who insisted she couldn't
swim was thrown fully clothed into the pool. I managed to dress
during the confusion caused by this and crept away unnoticed to
my room.

"There, to my dismay, an enormously tall redheaded girl in a
shiny wet bathing costume had passed out on my bed, which was
as soggy as if someone had been incontinent in it. There was no
point in attempting to revive her, really, for what I wanted to do
was have a nice sleep, and there wasn't much likelihood of that on
damp bed linen, but I gave her a sort of shake and made a few
encouraging 'wake-up' noises, whereupon she sat up straight,

opened her eyes, said, 'Dwight Deere Wiman' in an interrogatory way, and promptly passed out again.

"I was too sleepy to be angry, really. Clifton was still snoring away, and I went out into the corridor and began peering into other bedrooms and finally opened a door that revealed the largest single linen cupboard I had ever seen, stocked with eiderdowns and pillows and toweling bathrobes and the like. I made a kind of pallet on the carpeted floor with whatever came to hand, wrapped myself in an eiderdown and, closing the door first, went immediately to sleep."

It was Webb who found him and woke him about an hour later with the news that everybody was going over to a neighboring house to see a private showing of the newest *Thin Man* movie and then later on somewhere else for cocktails, and Noël rebelled. He pleaded illness, then fatigue, then boredom. He said he had religious scruples about keeping the sabbath holy and that watching movies on a Sunday, with or without William Powell and Myrna Loy in them, seemed to him a sacrilege. He said he had been promised a "quiet" weekend, and a quiet weekend was precisely what he meant to have, starting then and there.

Yet fifteen minutes later he was seated glumly in the back of Cobina's car again, trying to be pleasant.

"She handed me a steaming mug of tea which, when tasted, revealed that its bracing properties owed more to the region of Cognac than to the Isle of Ceylon, but it was warming and I drank it down quite happily. The icy roads were now covered with drifted snow, and the chauffeur had to stop for a time while he attached chains to the tires, and Cobina started to berate Clifton for some minor infraction of the house rules. This precipitated a quarrel between them that was filled with the wildest vituperation and most savage language ever heard outside of a barracks, and ended with Clifton's saying he wished he had gone to the Doubledays' instead, where the hospitality was gracious, the food edible, and the company had more tone. That was merely to be expected, he thought, because the Doubledays weren't *nouveau riche* and the Wrights *were*.

"I longed to leap out of the car and run for shelter somewhere, anywhere, but I didn't. The visibility was so poor that the chauffeur made a miscalculation of some kind and got us stuck in a great bank of snow so that he had to go on foot in search of help. It was growing dark and the heating in the car was inoperative, and Cobina told Clifton that if they were to freeze to death in that way she wanted him to know in her final hour that he was the only man she had ever truly loved; her husband meant nothing to her at all. I believe she made, through chattering teeth, some premature death-agony promise that if she ever got out of that arctic waste-land alive she would leave her husband at once and run off with Clifton to some tropical place where she was thinking of buying property. Clifton was so moved by this that he sniffled a good deal, and I suspected him for a moment of being perfectly sincere. But then the chauffeur came back with help in the form of a massive truck which obligingly pushed us out of our difficulties, and Clifton told her that after all his mother would never approve such an arrangement because of Cobina's inferior social position."

The cat fight continued until they were back at the Wright house again, where most of the swimming party had remained behind because of the condition of the roads and had been supplemented by a number of new faces arriving very late for the same reason. Among the latter were Monty Woolley with two young friends from Yale in tow, Tommy Manville with a showgirl he later married, and Lilly Daché, the milliner, who had lost a valuable earring and wanted everyone, Noël included, to help look for it.

There was also a deputation of what Noël called "nice young men who sell antiques" whose attentions were firmly fixed on the movie cowboys until the suggestion was made that Noël should sit down at the piano and entertain, whereupon he was the focus of everyone's undivided attention.

"Except for Grace Moore, who rescued me by singing 'Depuis le jour' from Louise while she refreshed herself from the mouth of a bottle of blended whiskey during the pauses. All the sofas and chairs being occupied, most of the visitors were distributed drunkenly about the floor, and Madame Daché was picking her way over the supine bodies in search of her bibelot and murmuring to herself in some tongue I didn't know, certainly not French.

"There was a fashion in those days for the 'progressive dinner,' which meant that one went to somebody's house for the first course, somewhere else for the soup and to a third place for the roast or whatever, and one such party had been planned for that night, with Cobina's house as the terminus for dessert and coffee. There was no way of knowing if the thing would go on as planned, as the telephone lines were down owing to the storm, and Cobina was hysterical with apprehension that there wasn't enough food in the larder to give dinner to those already there. I pointed out that there were enough chocolate gâteaux and ice cream to feed the King's regiment, and wondered aloud what could be keeping those fellows so long, but the sarcasm was totally wasted, and she went on about the nutritional properties of the lowly scrambled egg, which was what dinner would have to be.

"I settled down in the library briefly and listened to the wind howling and was trying to find Walter Winchell on the radio when one of the publishing tycoons came in to tell me about the manuscript of a novel he was reading which was a truly monumental achievement in that it had been written very stylishly and yet never once employed the letter 'e.' I amused myself by trying to think of even one sentence that was stylish but e-less and gave up when Madame Daché appeared with the announcement that Monty Woolley had concealed her earring in his beard and was now trying to make a joke of it when she knew perfectly well he had been trying to steal it all along.

"Boredom has only two avenues of release for me: one is rage and the other is oblivion achieved through great quantities of alcoholic drink, and I chose the latter. I fortified myself with several neat whiskies, and the events of the evening are blurred in my memory as a consequence. I do recall a confused dinner eaten at four or five big round tables, with people changing places every so often, and one of the Yale boys telling me that my plays were trivial and that I ought to see *Waiting for Lefty*.

"Additionally, this ass found my songs reminiscent, my acting affected, and thought that my darling Gertie Lawrence looked old on the stage. It is, of course, not the last straw that breaks the camel's back but the weight of the entire burden the beast has been carrying all along, and, realizing this, I stood up with exquisite dignity and recommended the boy to hell. And just in time, too, as another carload of progressive dinner people showed up looking like snowmen.

"There was a man in my bed, not yet quite asleep. I had never laid eyes on him before, yet there he was, large and middle-aged, wearing black satin pajamas and occupying a good two-thirds of the bed. I began by asking frigidly if he would mind going to his own room, and he replied reasonably that he couldn't do that because Grace was in there, probably with her chauffeur, and that he had been displaced. I pointed out that there were any number of other bedrooms vacant, but he assured me there weren't, as most of the other guests were snowbound and would be obliged to stay the night. Only the lucky, prudent ones had already claimed beds; the others without foresight would be sleeping on the living room floor.

"There was nothing else to do but to crawl in beside him. I switched off the lights, and instantly the snoring began, a snore like nothing I had ever heard, terminating in a kind of shrill whistle and interpolated by a wheezing *harrumph* that required the scrupulous attention of a specialist in asthma.

"I moved, then—somnambulistically, I'll admit—but I moved. I dressed. I scrawled a thank-you-and-good-bye note on some letter paper, placed it in an envelope on the desk and tiptoed out of the house with my overnight bag in hand, and no one saw me go."

An hour later he was picked up on the highway by a truck-driver and deposited at a railway station of the Long Island line, where he boarded a milk train and reached New York not long before dawn.

Two years later the short story appeared. Some of the gamier aspects of the weekend had to be rewritten to soothe the publisher's nerves about possible actions at law; "who shall be nameless" became an imperative and not a joke. Still, one or two of the characters became gradually recognizable to the cognoscenti. It was widely argued even then that the house described in the story was in reality one owned by the Doubledays, but Cobina Wright knew better, and vowed she would never forgive Noël for exposing her to such ridicule.

They did not meet again until after the war, when Mrs. Wright crossed a crowded room and wagged her forefinger at Noël in severe reproach.

"What was astonishing to discover," Noël said, "was that her outrage at my story had nothing whatever to do with the very unflattering delineation of her character as I had put it on paper. What *had* drawn blood, though, was a certain ambiguity about the man in the black satin pajamas I found in my bed. I did not learn until that very moment that it had been her husband. He had kept carefully out of sight throughout the whole nightmare. When I was able to assure her that nothing of an indelicate nature had occurred and that her husband had been solely interested in sleep and not in *me,* she sighed with relief and said that the whole matter was now forgotten, and we shook hands on it.

"It was a vague feeling of guilt, I suppose, and a feeling that my behavior may have been somewhat shabby, that made me agree to spend another weekend with her in the same house; that, and her assurances that the war had changed everything and that the servant shortage made it an impossibility to entertain in the grand style any longer. She said she couldn't even find a boy to mow the lawns no matter how much she offered.

"And so I went," Noël said, with a profound sigh. "And it will perhaps not come as a surprise to you, as it did to me—*exactly* the same house party was still going on!"

Graham Payn came in then from a shopping expedition, chilled to the bone, he said, and poured himself a cup of tea. I told him I had just heard about the weekend at Cobina Wright's.

"That must have taken all afternoon," he said, shooting a look at Noël that may have contained a reproach.

"I made a play out of it once," Noël said. "Called *House Party,* and it wasn't very good, I'm afraid. Too episodic, and all that stuff in the car simply can't be done convincingly on a stage. And, finally, it is no more than a very long anecdote, really."

It was to be five years before the subject of "making a play" out of *What Mad Pursuit?* was revived, and on that occasion it was I who suggested it, as a one-hour dramatization for English television, and as part of an anthology of similar dramatizations I had made of Noël's stories for the medium. My mind did not then run to the discovery of suitable dramatic material for the small screen, and the shock of the excellence of television in England was a sensation I would not experience for several years to come. Yet the germ of the idea that Noël's fiction ought to be dramatized was planted then and there, while Graham hurried on to the subject of my European jaunt, suggesting places to stay, good restaurants and fine hotels.

Then it was suddenly Noël's time to shoot Graham a look, and the reproach it contained was explicit. Any good, comfortable hotel ought to be adequate to my needs. He must at least have been gratified that St. Moritz was not on my itinerary.

"How long do you plan to stay in Venice?" he wanted to know.

"Five days, at the last counting," said I. (How wrong I was! It added up to something more like two years.)

"Three days in Venice is too much," he said, nearly quoting Henry James, "and a lifetime isn't enough. Where will you stay in London? You must have American friends living there."

"Oh, yes, but—"

"But you're going to a hotel instead."

"Well, I think I can come and go as I like more easily that way."

"Of course. An American sort of hotel?"

"Well—not exactly, no."

"Grosvenor House, I suppose."

"No. Actually—uh—Claridge's."

"I see. To be among the simple, unspoiled people there?"

I laughed. "Are there a lot of those people there?"

"Many. Completely unspoiled by their millions." He sighed wearily. "Well, enjoy it, dear boy. When we meet again you'll be much changed, for better or for worse."

8

The change was certainly for the better, but its progress was slow and difficult to chart in the memory. Certainly it did not commence for the first few months, when my time was divided between London and Paris in a milieu that was new and exciting and every day offered a surprise. One of the most delightful of these, arranged by an American friend, was a series of encounters with Vivien Leigh, who, within minutes of being introduced, treated me as if we had been lifelong friends. She was full of stories about Noël and had an uncanny knack for reproducing his unusual verbal rhythms with deadly accuracy. He had at the time begun work on a novel, and I wondered aloud what kind of novel it would be and what sort of story he would tell in it.

"I only know that it's set in Samolo," she said. "You know about Samolo, of course?"

I nodded. Samolo had been the setting for Noël's ill-fated operetta *Pacific 1860* which introduced Mary Martin to London audiences shortly after World War II. It was produced during the coldest winter London had seen in a decade in the unheated Drury Lane Theatre, whose program contained a geography-cum-history lesson in the form of a few paragraphs under the heading, "extract from a GUIDE TO SAMOLO." Evidently the tropical island that was the setting for the operetta was so insignificant a part of the Empire that it needed an introduction. The theatregoers learned, while their teeth chattered and their skins turned mauve in their orchestra seats, that it was of volcanic origin and had beaches of the finest white coral sand beside limpid lagoons and palm-fringed inlets. The program notes provided more pain than pleasure for the austerity-ridden Londoners, in whom southern longings are constant in the best of times. Under Aneurin Bevan's government all forms of foreign travel other than for official reasons were denied them.

Vivien said she had been deeply seized by southern longings that winter. Then the wife of Laurence Olivier, who was about to undertake an American tour with the Old Vic Theatre Company, she desperately wanted to get away somewhere that spring while Olivier was in New York, and after seeing an early performance of *Pacific 1860* with all of Gladys Calthrop's beguiling scenery, she knew exactly where she wanted to go. She invited Noël to lunch at the Ivy, the continuing magnet among restaurants for the London theatrical world, and it was at the same table where they lunched together that, thirteen years later, she told me all about it over a late supper.

"I knew Aneurin Bevan slightly, but Noël knew him better than I did, and I planned for him to speak to Bevan for me and say that I had been plagued all winter with this fearful cough and that my doctor would happily say I needed to be somewhere that was warm for a time.

"Noël and I picked over omelets made out of powdered eggs and dried *fines herbes* and he agreed to see what he could do. I wanted him to tell me more about Samolo, and, really, his enthusiasm for the place was so intense that it made it seem almost tropical *in here,* warmer than it is this evening, certainly.

"He kept trying to tell me about a play he was thinking of writing. He wanted to do it first in America, because he hadn't been represented there by anything new in such a long while, and he wanted me to consider whether I would be willing to commit myself to a long Broadway engagement with a subsequent London one and so on, and I was so tired and rheumy that for the moment I didn't want to think about work or plays or anything of the kind, and only with some persuasion did I manage to get him back on the subject of Samolo.

"Pendarla was where he thought I should stay, and he would give me a letter to the Governor's lady, who would look after me, but on no account to stay at Government House, which was uncomfortable and overrun with American visitors, and was unequivocally hideous anyway. I remember he said it looked like a gargantuan lilac blancmange. He knew a kind of villa set in a grove of poincianas that was sometimes for rent on a short-term basis. It had a verandah with banana-mesh tables and chairs and was overhung with jacaranda blossoms.

"Lady Alexandra Shotter was the name of the Governor's lady, and she was an absolute darling and a beauty to boot. I must on no account get into political discussions with an important native called Hali Alani, whose surname was the word for 'stars' in the Samolan language, because he had decidedly imperialist views but was sane on most other subjects. He was very handsome and fancied *all* Caucasian women, and so I had to watch my step. There was a chatterbox gossip called Mrs. Honey whom I could not possibly avoid at luncheons and dinners, but I must not encourage her. I was warned off the drinking water unless it had been boiled first. A certain fish whose name I forget was strongly recommended. I was ready to weep with anticipation and began dreaming of linen dresses and filmy chiffon gowns and palmetto fans.

"He would speak to Bevan first, of course, but knew it would be all right, and suggested flying to New York and from there to San Francisco, where I could book passage on a P. & O. liner for —I think it was Borneo, but I'm not sure. Once I had secured passage and all that, he would write ahead to Pendarla, make inquiries about the villa and so on, and impress upon Lady Shotter that I didn't want to be treated as a great celebrity and the less publicity about me the better.

"After lunch I went directly home—we lived in Chelsea near the Royal Hospital then—and rather dispiritedly looked through my wardrobe to see if there was anything wearable for the tropics, and of course there wasn't, but I soon remembered New York and my spirits rose again. I remembered all the marvelous shopping in New York and what the Americans call 'cruise clothes,' so I thought, well, not to worry, I'd spend a week there before going on to San Francisco. We had a well-stocked library in that house and I wandered downstairs and went directly for an old atlas. Search and search as I might, I couldn't *find* Pendarla anywhere, or even the Samolan group of islands on the map. But then I've always been hazy about longitudes and latitudes and the International Date Line and things like that, so I rang up the British Travel Association on an impulse, thinking perhaps they'd send me some literature. The man I talked to there was very sympathetic but he said he regretted to inform me that the island of Samolo was a figment of Noël Coward's imagination!''

Her porcelain features crinkled with merriment and she moved her head continuously from side to side as she described her reaction to having been "sent up within an inch of my life." I said I hadn't realized the extent to which Noël's fertile imagination might lead him.

"Oh, he can be a terrible tease," she said.

"It sounds like a rather cruel practical joke to me, and oddly very much out of character, at least as I know him."

"But don't you see what he was doing? The play he wanted to write and wanted to tell me about was to have Samolo as its setting. The people he mentioned were the characters who were going to be in it."

"This was—*South Sea Bubble?*"

"Yes. But it was called *Island Fling* then. When he talked about Lady Alexandra Shotter, the Governor's wife, that was the character he had in mind for *me,* although Gertie Lawrence said he had talked to her about it even before that. I was contracted elsewhere with a film or something and Claudette Colbert played her first in America, but I finally did play her, and for a long time, ten years later."

"Of course, you let him know that you'd found him out?"

"Of course. I rang him up in a fury and he merely chuckled in that maddening way he has, and that was that. As it happened, my doctor met Bevan at a dinner party and told him about my walking pneumonia and two weeks later I was in Jamaica, which was every bit as nice, really."

I told her about my special affection for Noël and something of its history, of the kind of parental authority he continued to assume with me whenever we were together.

"Yes, he sometimes does that with young people, because he takes such a great interest in everything, you see," Vivien said.

"He's always telling me to get out of New York and see people who have never heard of the theatre, and he doesn't at all approve of my staying at Claridge's here."

"Oh, you *have* to stay at Claridge's at least once. That's a part of life, too. God knows, Noël has lived a life of the greatest luxury, but has always managed to remain an essentially simple man."

"Yes, that's true, isn't it?" It was such a curious way of putting it that the truth of it struck me with full force.

"If he urges simplicity on you, or the simple life, rest assured he knows what he's doing. His advice is not given idly."

I did not embrace the simple life immediately, however. I had too long nourished the fantasy of seeing Europe in the fashion of my forebears, and I could now at last afford first-class travel and fine hotels. A heady disappointment was awaiting me later that year when it became abundantly clear that *Faster! Faster!* was not then, or ever, going to reach the stage. A contractual confusion with the film company had made it impossible for Carmen Capalbo to operate independently of them in producing the play as he wanted to do it; he rightly said that he could not continue with Hollywood moguls breathing over his shoulder every time he attempted to engage an actress for the leading role. Plans for the production were accordingly dropped, and, there being no professional reason for returning to New York in a hurry, I lingered in Venice, where the rhythm of life was soothing. I had begun to make notes for a story idea that was conceived as a screenplay and soon began to take shape as a novel.

From time to time there was news of Noël. His novel was completed and called *Pomp and Circumstance.* It was said to be as light as a book by Wodehouse. He was correcting proofs in the desert sunlight while appearing by night in a cabaret turn at a hotel in Las Vegas and had written a number of new songs for it, some of them among the best, it was said, he had ever done. A chance encounter with the late Harry Kurnitz, musicologist, playwright and wit, produced the news that Noël had written a musical comedy for the specific talents of Elaine Stritch and that it would be the first time a musical work of his would be seen in New York before it was presented in London.

With the manuscript of my finished novel, *Gondolier,* in my baggage I returned to New York again and read an advance copy of Noël's book, a delightful bit of fluff in the manner of Nancy Mitford, to whom it was dedicated. Shortly thereafter I was to attach myself unofficially to the production of the musical Harry Kurnitz had talked about, *Sail Away;* it was my single opportunity of observing Noël Coward in action, from the earliest stages of the production to its Broadway premiere. My interest in it was almost a proprietary one: Elaine Stritch was a good friend whom I longed to see succeed in a starring role, and Noël Coward was both a legend and a friend, to my mind the best confectioner of light entertainment in the world and one whose expertise would be fascinating and instructive to watch.

Noël brought the completed libretto, score and lyrics of *Sail Away* to Elaine in the early summer of 1961, presenting them to her like the cavalier with the silver rose in the Strauss opera. This kind of treatment was the one best calculated to elicit from Elaine a deep sense of responsibility and purpose, and it is certain that Noël had thought carefully beforehand exactly how he would proceed with her; she had earned a reputation in New York theatrical circles for being erratic, quarrelsome and unreliable. Yet even her critics acknowledged that she was among the most gifted actresses and song stylists of the time if only she could be made tractable and not permitted to seize the reins of a show, as it was —inaccurately—reported she had done not long before.

He called her "Stritchie" from the outset. The paternal role he played with her was one with which I was more than familiar, though it manifested itself differently and achieved quite different results. A certain hard-boiled manner she employed when not working was suddenly absent; she resumed all the *jeune fille* mannerisms that are habitual with her when she feels surrounded by loving admirers.

All the ardent swains or sycophantic suitors of her company in the world did not count for much when it was Noël Coward who was at her feet in worship, with a gleaming offering of a spectacular part in a new show especially manufactured for her talents like a bespoke garment. She wore bouffant skirts and put ribbons in her hair and hummed little tunes to herself as if she were genuinely in love for the first time. Her fondness for the grape was displaced by a taste for hops, and her friends buzzed with pleasure at the substitution of Heineken's for Dom Perignon. One man-of-the-moment was sent packing and a new one appeared. Appointments made were no longer broken with a lame excuse at the last moment, old friendships were revived after an embarrassing interruption, and the ego-nourishing dullards who were present from dinner till dawn were banished to wherever they had come from in the first place. She herself articulated the transformation in the plainest words: "It's the *new* Elaine Stritch, dear," she told me in her four A.M. voice. "It's Noël *Coward's* Elaine Stritch."

She wanted, and did not get, star billing above the title. Her argument was theatrically sound: she had received co-star billing in *Goldilocks,* and to have her name slip under the title was a reduction of eminence that minimized her importance to the show and would certainly be a succulent topic for the theatrical community to chew over. Noël said that if the critics' notices warranted it, her name would go above the title after the opening night. She was obliged to settle for that.

But the billing question continued to plague Noël as rehearsals progressed. Apart from Elaine, the company of *Sail Away* was a motley conglomeration of well-known featured players, promising newcomers and half-forgotten old-timers. The ladies among them were nervously concerned about the order in which their names would appear on the billboards, the marquee and the program and in the advertising. Their eminence had to be taken into account, and there was no better form of accounting for it than by rewarding them with a prominent place directly under Elaine's name in the largest possible type of lettering. Alice Pearce and Margalo Gilmore were perfectly content to be billed as they were, but a young ingenue who sang prettily and danced expertly and to whom Noël had taken a strong dislike because of her habit of rephrasing her lines didn't want to be lost in the crowd of featured players and demanded something a little different for herself. She proposed that her name appear in type that was at least seventy-five percent of the size used for Elaine's. Moreover, she wanted it to appear at the very bottom of the listing of the other performers, to be set apart in a kind of box, and to be preceded by the word "And."

Elaine, whose early friendliness towards the girl had now settled into a kind of polite acceptance, demanded to know if Noël was going to accede to her billing demands. "Are you seriously thinking," she asked him, "of putting that girl's name in a box? Preceded by the word *'And'*?"

"I will put her name in a box," replied Noël, "only if it is preceded by the word *'But.'* "

Sail Away had originated in Noël's mind as a kind of revue, an amalgam of songs and skits with a unifying theme, that of a

Mediterranean cruise on board a Cunarder, calling at Tangier, Taormina and Piraeus, its point of origin being New York. Elaine appeared as Mimi Paragon, the cruise hostess, a dynamic shepherdess for a flock of variegated passengers and their numerous children, dogs and cameras; bitten hard by a history of romantic disillusionments, she was twice shy of the youngish playboy on board who was aggressively attentive to her. Noël had written a half dozen songs for this character, all of them relying on verbal gymnastics for their humor: one was an "alphabet song," sung with a group of children, that was a wicked parody of "Do-Re-Mi" from *The Sound of Music;* another had a lyric composed entirely of the kind of idiotic and useless phrases to be found in the slim volumes intended to facilitate a rapid mastery of foreign languages; a third was an unequivocal masterpiece, "Why Do the Wrong People Travel?" There were love songs, too, and these were distributed about equally among the other principals, two ballads having been written specifically for the lovely soprano of a noted American opera star. Noël had not attempted anything even half so ambitious for longer than a decade, and on the first day of rehearsals a sense of something very important and of the highest quality informed the mood of the participants.

Elaine began to sing her phrase-book song, the first line of which is "When the tower of Babel fell . . ." She pronounced the name of the biblical city to rhyme with "scrabble."

Noël stopped her. "It's *'bayble,'* Stritchie."

"It's what?"

"Bayble. It rhymes with 'table.' "

"I've **always** said 'babble,' Noël. Everyone says 'babble.' It means mixed-up language, doesn't it? Gibberish? It's where we get 'babble' from. I never even *heard* it pronounced the way you just said it. It's *babble,* and that's the way I'm saying it."

She stood firm, arms akimbo. She waited. "Babble," she said again.

"That's a fabble," said Noël.

Round one went to Noël, as did each succeeding one. There is nothing cerebral about Elaine; her acting is entirely instinctive, and its quicksilver nature is achieved without reference to her intellect or suspected unconscious motivations. She simply walks on the stage and *does* what seems right to her to do, and it accordingly seems right to everyone else. Behind her back, Noël had the highest praise for her. "I have never seen her put a foot wrong," he told me in confidence, and then added, "on*stage*, I mean."

I interested myself in the fortunes of *Sail Away* as studiously as if I were its chief investor. It had a quality of sophisticated fun that was not common to the musical shows of the period, a stylishness and grace that reminded me of the Rodgers and Hart and Cole Porter musicals of the thirties I had enjoyed so thoroughly when I was a boy. If its story was insubstantial, it was no flimsier than that of *Roberta* or *Babes in Arms,* and its score was rich, full of novelties, and spectacularly up-to-date. I attended rehearsals, which were conducted in a relaxed and civilized manner, and marveled at Noël's use of an iron fist with a velvet touch; he was superbly in command of everything.

A beautiful little girl who looked four years younger than she actually was exhibited the qualities of a scene-stealer three times her age during the song Elaine sang in the children's nursery. Her Goldilocks charm was distracting, and someone suggested to Noël that, in the interests of keeping the audience's attention fixed on Elaine and the song itself, it might be better if the child were eliminated from the scene altogether. Noël rubbed his upper lip with his forefinger and remembered an old theatrical rule. He said something about turning a disadvantage into an advantage. He called for the tiny enchantress to join him in the orchestra, where he was seated.

He told her he was going to teach her how to smoke, opened his cigarette case and gave her a cigarette. She accepted it gracefully, put it in her mouth and waited for Noël to give her a light as if she were accustomed to smoking at least two packs a day. With a kind of mock *politesse* and in a husky, sexy voice, she asked him, "Do you mind if I smoke?"

He concealed his astonishment with the words, "Not if it's tobacco."

Puffing away, the little girl returned to the stage. Noël instructed Elaine to turn, at one point during the song, observe the child smoking, react strongly, and move to take the cigarette away from her. The child was told to run, then, for the exit. It was a splendid solution. It would satisfy the audience's wish to single out the girl for attention, appreciate her briefly, and remove her from the scene at once so that Elaine might get on with the song, secure in the knowledge that she was the sole focus of interest. It also never failed to get a healthy laugh in performance.

The late Alice Pearce was a funny lady both onstage and off. Her role in the musical was not a long one and did not provide many opportunities for the extravagant clowning that was her forte; moreover, having several times been a show-stopper with comedy songs in other productions, she deplored the fact that Noël had not written a song for her to display her erratic soprano. From time to time this lack had been pointed out to Noël, who said, "There simply isn't *room!*" and she had to be content with that. One hot July Sunday afternoon, the day before the production was set to leave for its trial run in Boston, the show was performed from beginning to end without interruption before a handful of invited spectators. It went remarkably smoothly, all things considered, and very much as planned except for a series of novel exits made by Miss Pearce that had never been rehearsed and that surprised the members of the company every bit as much as it did Noël. She had a number of brief scenes throughout the action, each one terminating with a slow and plodding march on uncertain legs from one side of the stage to the other. That afternoon each of her exits was embellished with an operatic delivery of the first line of one of Noel's famous songs, from "I'll See You Again" to "Mad About the Boy," an interpolation that was not at all the amusing invention she had hoped it would be. There were audible groans from the auditorium and here and there a shocked, nervous laugh. But Noël smiled benignly on the proceedings and showed nothing of his displeasure. He reserved that until the very end, when, after hearing the usual theatrical courtesies from those who had seen the run-through, he went directly backstage and climbed the stairs to Miss Pearce's dressing room.

It was an aspect of Noël I had never seen or, more precisely, heard. The entire backstage area of the Broadhurst Theatre rang with vituperation and abuse. The word "unprofessional" was used several times. He had searched his long memory and in it he could find, he said, no single example of equivalent insubordination or impudent mockery. It was he who had insisted on her being cast in the role over the objections of others because it was rumored that she needed the job. Deliberately to introduce snatches of his songs from other shows as if he were apologizing for the quality of the new songs he had written for *Sail Away,* and at the same time reminding the audience of his past successes, was expressive of a vulgarity and self-advertisement unparalleled in his experience. There may have been tears, for Noël's voice reduced its volume suddenly. Most of the company stood about with looks of deep embarrassment and worry: Miss Pearce was a great favorite with them all. I remember the scene as having made me very nervous, and anxious for Noël. When he came downstairs again he had a pale, tired look, and Graham Payn and Cole Lesley, Noël's secretary, solicitously guided him to a waiting limousine outside.

I was fond of Alice Pearce, and I felt she had been merely unwise in what she had done. Her interpolations had been a one-performance-only matter, born of frustration and nerves. Perhaps she felt that Noël had forgotten how very funny she could be when she broke into mad vocal flights in full operatic delivery that were always just a quarter-tone off key. It had seemed, however, to everyone that she was making a mockery of the Metropolitan soprano who was one of the stars, as well as rebuking Noël for not providing her with the comedy song she had long expected he would write specifically for her.

Her hopes for such a bonus were permanently dashed that afternoon. Had she introduced snatches of familiar music by Puccini or Verdi, the matter might have been easy to resolve. But she had chosen to parody four or five of Noël's most beloved songs and, for her final embellishment, elected to have some fun with one of the most touching lines he ever wrote: "All I have is a talent to amuse," which his biographer, Sheridan Morley, understood to be Coward's final estimate of himself. Alice Pearce had unwittingly touched an exposed nerve.

The episode was misunderstood. Many in the company, particularly the singers and dancers of the chorus, sided with the comedienne and were unable to conceal their championship of her. One or two of them may have said a few ill-chosen words on the subject to the stage manager or other representative of the management. The disagreement was magnified into a *cause* that was soon said to be a feud. Noël always disliked backstage warfare, and stood above the battle like a disinterested spectator, but in this fray he was nominated as the principal belligerent. It was largely for this reason, I think, that for the rest of the theatrical life of *Sail Away* he never exchanged more than simple courtesies with Alice.

Cole Lesley was, for me, a newcomer to the scene, although he had been a fixture of the various Coward households for years. He had begun as a manservant and functioned as one for Noël until Mrs. Lorn Lorraine, who managed every detail of Noël's professional life from a small house in Belgravia, one day observed, "Coley is better-read than all of us put together." Noël acted upon the remark instantly, and elevated Coley to the role of private secretary. A small, spare man with a sunny disposition and a highly developed sense of humor, he gave the impression at first sight of being in complete authority and that nothing awkward or disagreeable could cross Noël's path so long as Coley was nearby to forestall it. He was, of course, much, much more than a troubleshooter, and was valued by everyone who knew him as a reassuring adjunct of Noël's daily life. Throughout the weeks to come, Coley was to be a tower of strength and gentle persuasion, as he and Graham in concert would scan the horizon for heavy weather ahead and run interference for Noël like players on a football field.

Because, as was evident immediately on the opening night in Boston, there was something very wrong with *Sail Away*. The audiences seemed to be impatient with it, with the romantic entanglements of the opera star, the playboy, and the younger couple, and responded warmly only to the energetic dancing and the comedy songs Elaine sang. The effect of her presence in the show was sore-thumblike: at three different points during the first act and again in the second the stage would come to blazing life with her exalted mummery, only to dim again while the various love stories

were dispiritedly enacted and sung about. The billing-hungry ingenue was mostly to blame for the lifelessness at the center of the
juvenile affair; her opposite number, Grover Dale, had charm and
energy and a winning stage presence. There was nothing at all to
engage the affections of the audience in the mature romance,
which was stilted and stale and might have wandered in by mistake
from a deservedly forgotten operetta. The two excellent singers
concerned in it could not have brought reality to it even had they
known how to act. Noël, in the audience, would sometimes shield
his eyes from the glare of dullness they brought with them every
time they walked on stage.

There was, fortunately, time for something to be done, for
mistakes to be corrected, the story revised, the singers replaced.
But four weeks of the six-week pre-Broadway tour, in Boston and
Philadelphia, were consumed with uncertainty and discursive planning, trial and error. Noël, as captain of the ship, and Joe Layton,
who staged the dances and musical numbers, as his first mate,
didn't know what to make of the weather and proceeded with
caution rather than daring in steering their course. Time was running short. A dance number was changed here, a song repositioned
there; but the revisions were merely decorative and not structural.
The critics in Philadelphia were spare with their praise except for
Elaine. One of them omitted to mention the name of the opera
singer. In New York the gossips predicted that the show would be
abandoned before it reached Broadway, a view that survived even
the postponement of its scheduled opening night at the Broadhurst
Theatre.

After the opening performance in Philadelphia, Noël and a
group of friends repaired to a restaurant Elaine had caused to
remain open long after its normal business hours; the owners were
old and valued friends of hers. The night was as hot and airless as

only a September night in Philadelphia can be; the theatre had been stifling and the audience uncomfortable and desultory in their response. At the interval I had heard a woman say that she had seen Noël and that he looked old and tired and was it any wonder that the show was the same? The restaurant we went to was long and narrow as a railway carriage, but it was wonderfully cool and the cold supper was sumptuous. Noël consumed his salad before he said a word, and asked for more. His dissatisfaction with the evening's reception was evident to me; there was perplexity and worry in his face and he often appeared to be thinking of something else while the conversation buzzed around him. The captain knew that the ship was in danger of foundering. When a chair beside him became vacant I went over and sat down next to him.

His tone was confidential. "If I have learned one thing from this experience, and so late in life, it is that my besetting sin is to be seduced by a beautiful voice. If that voice is a fine, clear soprano the more am I enslaved by it. Exceptional baritones have a similar effect.

"Never, never, never, dear boy, allow it to happen to you. The great voices should remain forever at La Scala or wherever they are paid best. I promise you, and everyone within earshot, that I will never again engage a singer to play a part that requires even the slightest suggestion of histrionic ability. From now on, it will only be actors who can 'get away' with a song, or even talk it if absolutely necessary."

It was in his mind then, I knew, to replace the soprano and that he would be the one to tell her so. My sympathy went out to the lady; she was beautiful as well as accomplished and had a very sweet nature. But her shortcomings as an actress were too great; she would have to be dismissed as quickly as possible and some-one else would have to be engaged who, even if her singing was of a different order, could at least act the part. I tried to say something heartening. "Well, Noël," I said, "I really think that of all male singers, my personal favorites were always Gene Kelly and Fred Astaire."

The reply was like lightning. "You're *so* right. My favorite dancers were always Nelson Eddy and Jeanette MacDonald."

The quip delivered, he resumed the telling of confidences. He had no idea of finding someone to step into the soprano's part. I looked at him in amazement. He smiled his Mahatma smile. He was going to combine, he said, the soprano's character with that of the cruise hostess and, please, to be quiet about it, as Elaine knew nothing of the plan. In this way two of the best songs in the show would then be sung by Elaine, and she would not be missing from the stage for very long stretches at a time. Her augmented role would afford her the opportunity of achieving a *tour de force;* it would, unquestionably, thrust her into the firmament, where she had so richly deserved to be for so long a time, among the very few other astral beings already fixed there.

"Will you put her name above the title?" I whispered.

"If the notices warrant," he said. "But *only* then."

It sounded a revolutionary scheme to me, and a good one. The amount of work to be done in the span of a few short weeks was prodigious, but a prodigy was on hand to execute it. I disagreed with the lady during the interval: he looked neither old nor tired to me. For a man who had, in his early years, boasted of the speed with which his plays were written, the prospect of immediate surgery on *Sail Away* ought not to have been dismaying. But Noël had never rewritten extensively at the same time as the work being revamped was playing nightly performances. Generally, a show is rewritten scene by scene, the new scene is rehearsed by day and inserted in that evening's performance. The task with *Sail Away* was to rewrite the book scenes from beginning to end, combining the two parts played by Elaine and the soprano, so that the story was entirely different from what had been played before. It was impossible to insert even one scene at a time so long as the soprano continued as the inamorata of the young man who was so soon to switch his affections to Elaine. Accordingly, it was two weeks before the new version could take to the stage, and there remained only ten performances before the opening night in New York in which to perfect it, polish it, time the comedy lines, and allow the actors to grow confidently into their parts.

It was not enough time. The character of Mimi Paragon, straightforward and uncompromising, sassy and droll, as Elaine had created her underwent a sea-change. Some of the new writing called for a soft femininity to show through the hard-boiled exterior; an especial vulnerability was wanted for the song that had come to her secondhand, "Something Very Strange." Six weeks of playing a part one way needed six more weeks to adjust the character to the new situation in which she found herself. The writing had been performed with haste and lacked Noël's customary polish; consequently, as the show was performed before preview audiences in New York, no two performances were alike. Noël was continually cutting a word here, truncating a scene there, repositioning the actors in order to smooth the rougher edges. In hindsight he was to agree that all the Philadelphia performances should have been canceled following the opening there, thus permitting intensive rehearsals; the suggestion had been made earlier but rejected as economically out of the question.

Elaine was uneasy before the premiere performance in New York. The show now rested squarely upon her shoulders, and she gave a fine imitation of Atlas to conceal her uncertainty. She complained of insufficient rehearsal and a wig that gave her a splitting headache.

Halfway into the first act, following the comedy song of "useful phrases," Noël had written a delicate scene played on the upper deck of the cruise liner under a Mediterranean moon. The young playboy appeared there to seize the opportunity of a moment alone with Elaine, who was airing a dozen dogs on tandem leads in this unvisited part of the ship. The scene began with the line: "We must be approaching land. There's a definite change in the air." Elaine's reply was, "Soon you'll be able to see the lighthouse at Algeciras."

Before her suitor entered the scene, however, opening-night nerves attacked one of the poodles; the dog chose the center of the stage to relieve himself spectacularly. The audience roared. The playboy entered and was obliged to wait for quiet before he delivered his line. At the mention of "a change in the air" the audience exploded with laughter and applauded. Confusion mounted onstage; the young man found it difficult to conceal his merriment. Elaine knew that the audience must be restored to order in some way: the whole love story depended on its appreciation of the scene to be played. But the situation had made the spectators unruly; it would be best to wait a little until they became more temperate. Unwisely, she elected to improvise a few lines. Looking over her dozen charges as if she had raised them from puppyhood, she said, "I can't even remember which one *did* that."

The fate of *Sail Away,* as far as the critics were concerned, was sealed then and there. From that point on, the relationship between the cruise hostess and her rich suitor was understood to be comic. Lines never previously suspected of being amusing were greeted with rich laughter. The outcome of the romance lost its important element of ambiguity: whatever happened, whether the pair married, separated, or went through life together like two buddies, the denouement was going to be funny. A lovely, wistful scene of renunciation Noël had written to be played just before the final curtain elicited titters rather than tears. Elaine took a number of curtain calls by herself to prolonged applause, yet the total effect of the evening was severe disappointment. Brave faces were put on; the play was said to be an undisputed triumph; phrases of congratulation were commonplace backstage. There was still an elaborate after-theatre party to be endured before the mask of gaiety could be dropped to reveal the frustration beneath.

The producers had arranged a gala supper at Sardi's East for a hundred and fifty guests; a Pinkerton man was at the entrance to forestall the entry of the uninvited. One who had not been bidden to come, through a possible oversight, was the late James Thurber, and he protested so loudly at the door, repeating his name in mounting fury to the detective who was denying him admission, that someone of the restaurant's staff made it his responsibility to find a place for the blind humorist at the bar and promised to seat him at a table as soon as he could make room.

The assembly consisted largely of the show-business aristocracy and representatives of mining fortunes from the West whose money had financed *Sail Away:* the Lunts, infrequently visible at large gatherings, dignified the occasion; Miss Fontanne seemed a royal visitor indeed, in gray watered silk with a lace fichu in her hair to which it was fixed with diamond clips. I sat with Noël at a large round table next to the dance floor; above an extravagant centerpiece of autumn flowers Marlene Dietrich's eyes watched over him like an attentive nursemaid. He was hungry, and said so, and what he wanted was a big plate of hot soup. The plans for supper had not taken into account the possibility of his wanting something other than the set meal. If there was soup in the larder, and the waiter was by no means sure that there was, it would have to be heated. The waiter foresaw a great drama in the kitchen when he presented this order to the chef. Some one of the second chefs would have to attend to the heating of the soup, taking him away from his appointed job of grilling steaks. Wouldn't Mr. Coward settle for some nice vichyssoise? No, interposed Miss Dietrich, Mr. Coward wanted *hot* soup; he had eaten nothing since noon. He had said mock turtle, but any other good, thick soup would do, *hot* vichyssoise, even. The waiter looked stricken. Miss Dietrich looked about for Vincent Sardi, who was not in the immediate vicinity. She took the waiter into her confidence with a tone that seemed to invite him to some unspecified future entanglement with her. She said if he would bring out an apron to protect her dress she would go into the kitchen and heat the soup herself.

The waiter saw the security of his good job threatened; he would, he said, attend to the heating of the soup *himself.*

Elaine had her own table next to Noël's, where she was surrounded by relatives and close friends. The Dom Perignon wasn't cold enough for her; a highball glass was crammed with ice cubes, and the wine frothed over the rim of the glass when it was poured. Spilled wine to this day causes Elaine to dip two fingers of her right hand into it and fashion the sign of the cross with them, anointing the foreheads of everyone nearby in turn. She reached over my shoulder to place a drop of champagne on Noël's brow and then on mine. "We must be approaching land," she said in a deep baritone; "there's a definite change in the air." Noël smiled grimly.

The soup appeared, a rich minestrone with the look of a steaming swamp. Noël regarded it suspiciously and began munching a breadstick. James Thurber was at his side then, irritably demanding to know why he had not been seated for his supper. He refused to be treated in a shabby way. He was America's greatest humorist, as Noël was Britain's. Noël had proved that much once again, and conclusively, for Thurber that evening, as Thurber had been proving it to every educated reader of the English language since Hector was a pup. Here was America's acknowledged humorist par excellence in the same room with his opposite number from England, and the former was hurt that he hadn't been included in the latter's party. How many people were seated at Noël's table, and who were they, anyway? Was there no room for him there?

"Isn't there *one* chair vacant? I'm *blind,* you know."

"Not one, Jimmy. I don't know who did the seating arrangements."

I started to yield my seat, but Noël restrained me with a firm grasp of my forearm. "Go and sit down over there on the other side of the dance floor; the waiter will guide you, and I'll come over and join you in a moment. I just want to get some soup in me first."

"Are you *snubbing* me, Noël?"

"No, I'm starving, Jimmy. I must get this soup into me. Let the waiter show you where to sit and I'll be with you."

The waiter took Thurber's arm gently, and, for a moment, the danger of an embarrassing scene was averted. Noël ran his spoon through the minestrone.

"He may be quite ill," he said in an undertone.

"He is certainly very drunk," said I.

"That's more than alcohol, that kind of rage. He always used to be so gentle."

"The blind are often rather cranky," I said.

"Irritable, yes, because they are disorientated. Is his wife with him?"

"I don't see her."

"I shall go over and sit with him when I have eaten this."

Whispers circulated through the company like a spreading brush fire. Word of the *New York Times* critic's review was distributed like handbills among them; the show was said to be old-fashioned and lackluster and only fitfully amusing. A four-piece group of musicians put a lot of enthusiasm into some forgettable dance music then, as grilled steaks were served and red wine was poured. A microphone was connected and set near the band in the expectation that someone would sing.

"The smiles are less broad, suddenly," said Noël. "That means either Kerr or Atkinson is bad."

An emissary of the management brought him whispered news; he nodded and thanked him and told him to get himself something to eat.

"They're both bad," he said, as if it were the future of a show somebody else had written, composed and directed that was thus sentenced. "I must go over and sit with Jimmy Thurber."

He rose from his seat to do so at the same moment that Thurber seized the microphone on the dance floor and blew into it to see if it worked. Noël sat down at once.

Thurber launched into a discursive and only partly intelligible wave of abuse from which no one, and most especially Noël, was spared. He, Thurber, was the greatest of all American humorists, he said, or had been regarded as such by every thinking person for two generations; tonight all that had changed: he was now the greatest humorist in the English language. What he had heard from the stage that evening shamed and embarrassed him in its pale and reminiscent mediocrity; he had heard nothing funny in it, and, though blind, as everyone must surely know, he had *seen* nothing funny in it. And who the hell was Noël Coward, anyway, to snub *him* and not invite him to the party? And, having forgotten to invite him to the party, why was it he had been refused permission even to say hello to Coward? The truth was that Noël was *past* it, and had always been a snob, and the evening's fiasco was ample proof of it. The matter was that the show was anti-American and simply went to show what Coward had always thought of Yankees: all of us gathered there in celebration of this *fop* were objects of his scorn, ignorant colonials who were not fine enough to sit at his table.

At a signal from someone, the band started to drown out Thurber's voice; somebody else disconnected the microphone; Noël cupped his right hand over his ear as if straining to hear every word. Two men took Thurber in hand and shepherded him away. A gloom settled like fine rain on the party. Elaine wanted to know what had gone wrong.

"I think Jimmy is seriously ill," said Noël, "not drunk."

Later, a handful of us prolonged the mood of discouragement and regret with an artificial show of high spirits at Noel's pied-à-terre on East 54th Street. Elaine had brought along a bottle of Dom Perignon which she guarded closely. Cole Lesley moved about, pouring drinks efficiently with a benign smile. Noël read through his opening night telegrams and passed them, one by one, to Coley. Graham Payn answered the telephone every few minutes and reassured the callers that Noël was fine, was taking it well, was not in the least bit distressed, and had always believed it was essentially an "audience show."

Graham was right. Audiences who found their way to it that winter left the theatre humming the tunes. Noël sipped scotch-and-soda highballs and teased Elaine and told her that the trouble with her hair was that there was too much of it. Any disparagement of her appearance is an invitation to open warfare with her, but the false gaiety of the occasion was too tenuous to admit of arguments, and Elaine fully understood that Noël was not really talking about her hair. He coolly recalled other disastrous opening nights and shook his head in wonderment at how many of them there had been. He turned to me.

"Would you know where the Thurbers live?" he asked.

I didn't know. My impression was that they lived somewhere in the country but stayed at the Algonquin when they were in New York.

"It's too late to ring now, but I must talk to Mrs. Thurber first thing tomorrow."

Elaine was surprised, she said, that he would want to communicate with Thurber ever again after the way the man had behaved earlier.

"Stritchie, that wasn't Jimmy Thurber talking that way. That was something horrid in his brain. I have known people with brain tumors to behave that way. They invariably rage like Lear at whatever is close to hand. I want to be sure that Mrs. Thurber knows the seriousness of what is happening to him and that he is having the proper medical supervision, poor man."

The afternoon papers the following day carried more unfavorable reviews of *Sail Away;* they also printed the news that James Thurber had suffered a cerebral hemorrhage during the early morning hours.

The critical response to the show did not justify lifting Elaine's name to a majestic prominence above the title on the marquee, and in the alphabetical listings of Broadway attractions in the newspapers the show was advertised as "Noël Coward's *Sail Away*" without reference to its players. Noël remained in New York only until the songs had been recorded for an album and then flew to Jamaica for a rest.

9

Sail Away had a profitable run in London, but it did not greatly enhance Noël's reputation. Elaine Stritch received the kind of critical acclaim that is normally reserved for dramatic actresses in one of the great Shakespearean roles, and it was on the strength of this praise rather than on the merits of the show itself that it had a respectable run. There had long been critical indifference to Coward's works. His last play, *Waiting in the Wings,* had been dismissed two years earlier as sentimental and badly carpentered, and now it was his song-writing that was no longer up to standard. His experimentation with new rhythms and untypical lyrics was seen as a futile effort to change his style and conform to the contemporary taste, and implicit in the evaluations of him was the suggestion that he was as outmoded as Ivor Novello or Victor Herbert.

Always sanguine in the face of critical brickbats, Noël undertook at once to write another musical, an ambitious operetta version of Terence Rattigan's sentimental comedy, *The Sleeping Prince,* set in London at the time of the coronation of Edward VII. He wanted to call it *Passing Fancy,* one of the happiest titles he ever found in a long career of witty labels for his works, but the Broadway management prevailed and the show was called *The Girl Who Came to Supper.*

Difficulties dogged the enterprise from the outset. The casting of the two leading roles was far from inspired, and a supporting comedienne from the London music halls who had never before appeared in New York performed theatrical larceny with a couple of street songs in the first act in such a way that there was no hope of restoring the audience's interest in the central story afterwards. Advance publicity concerning the show, moreover, aroused such anticipation of excellence that only a miracle could have satisfied. Yet it received an ecstatic press in Philadelphia, where it opened, and the engagement was played to capacity houses. Pleased but puzzled by the response to what he felt was in need of considerable tinkering, Noël seized the opportunity of a week's rest and sun at Blue Harbour, his house in Jamaica, before supervising the show's transfer to New York. But the respite turned out to last only a few hours, as he explained when I saw him the following week. The day of his arrival at the island retreat was Friday, November 22, 1963, the date of the assassination of John F. Kennedy.

"My shock," he said, "when a servant came out on the terrace to tell me was immense. I had known the President slightly— we used to talk together about old Hollywood movies, of which his knowledge was actually encyclopedic. My eyes filled with tears as I gazed out at the sea and at my red jeep parked in the driveway. From down the hill I could hear the weekend festivities of the natives—the laughter and the shouting and the metallic sound of their steel drums. All I could think of was how inappropriate it was for them to be having such a carry-on at such a sad time, when a man who had done so much to aid in the social advancement of their race, not only in his own country but everywhere else, it seemed to me, had just been struck down by an assassin."

We were sitting in a little bar adjacent to the Broadway Theatre, where the musical was preparing for its New York opening. The atmosphere of the city was very changed, like a community where a curfew had just been enforced. The streets were nearly deserted, the restaurants empty, and a gloom had settled on the populace that the electric day of the theatre district could do nothing to brighten. The sense of a great national tragedy was everywhere, and Noël's eyes were again moist as he referred to it.

"Would the Jamaicans know the name?" I asked. "Did they know who Kennedy was?"

"I'm coming to that. As I sat there thinking about the grief that all America must be feeling, the hard reality of show business came rushing at me on all cylinders. Until last Saturday in Philadelphia, the first twenty minutes of *The Girl Who Came to Supper* concerned an assassination attempt! There could certainly be no joy or entertainment to be had from the rest of the show with such a portentous beginning, in the light of what had just happened. The enormity of the effect the tragedy would have on the American people, possibly for many years to come, was blindingly clear to me. It was perfectly obvious that there could now be no mention of an attempted assassination in the show. Even the music for the opening scenes would have to be changed. I threw a few things in a bag, hopped into my red jeep and sped down the hill on the way to the airport, hoping there was a flight to Philadelphia and that I could get on it.

"Now, down the hill there is a kind of dance-hall-cum-rum-parlor, often so crowded that the customers spill out into the road. There they were, drinking and carousing, and I heard cries of 'Heah come Mistah Coward,' as they cleared the way a little so that my jeep might pass. Instead, I brought it to a stop.

" 'Be quiet!' I shouted at them in one of my more imperious tones. Never having had anything but the warmest courtesy from me in all the years I've spent among them, they were shocked and fell instantly silent. I can't remember exactly what I said, but I know I made a kind of speech reproaching them for their unfeeling behavior in the wake of an international tragedy, and reminded them that the fallen hero had been their champion, and so on, and they gazed at me solemnly like mischievous children caught in the act.

"Feeling that I had made my point effectively and that they would all now retire with dignity to their homes, I pressed down hard on the pedal, only to find the gears in reverse, and I backed up the hill quickly with my face revealing my surprise. They whooped with laughter. Jamaicans have a sense of humor that responds very strongly to the inappropriate."

I laughed as well. His own expression changed to one of merriment briefly, and he nodded at the curiously inevitable way the comic has of rearing its head in the middle of the tragic. "I shifted the gears," he went on, "and drove haughtily down the hill, their laughter and music continuing in my ears all the way. It may have been the worst exit I ever made!"

Then his expression turned grave again. The overwhelming sense of mourning that informed every moment of daily life in the weeks following the assassination merely accentuated a strange melancholy I found in him that evening. He was deeply troubled about the show, and, having just seen it that evening for the first time, there was very little I could say in the way of encouragement. Apart from the two rowdy songs sung by the Cockney performer, the music was not at all memorable, as much of *Sail Away* had been, and the lyrics lacked his customary wit and polish. There was an air of fatigue about the whole enterprise, and a strong sense of *déjà vu* that could never be corrected. He knew it more surely than I did, and seemed exhausted with the knowledge. It was the first time I had seen him put anything less than the very best face on things, the first time he had seemed to me depleted of energy. The light in the bar had an unflattering bluish cast that clearly showed his age: he would be sixty-four years old in a few weeks.

I had spent most of that year in London and now was planning to live there on a permanent basis; I would be returning at Christmas. He approved of the decision, and expressed his fears about the dramatic changes he foresaw in American life resulting from the events of the previous week. It would, perhaps, be better to absent oneself from it all. He himself would spend the winter in Jamaica and the summer in Switzerland, and visit London from time to time, where, of course, we would meet.

"Anarchy," he said, as we left the bar together. "And it will only breed further anarchy." I hailed a taxi for him. He squinted up at the marquee of the theatre, where the lights had now been dimmed. "*Passing Fancy* would have been *such* a better title!"

It was a year and a fortnight before I saw him again.

London was now familiar ground to me, and soon I was embarked on a new and different kind of writing assignment, in a field I had promised myself would never be comfortable for me. Bored and irritated by the quality of American television, I had not been prepared for the excellence of the British equivalent—what

Noël dignified as "the minor screen": its daring to explore new techniques and the high standards of its productions, which employed the finest English theatrical talents in every department, and without reference to the dictates of commercial enterprise. I wrote several original comedies that were impeccably produced and handsomely received, and learned that, in England at any rate, the television play is a unique form, continuous neither with the craft of the cinema nor that of the theatre. It is, as someone neatly put it, only "radio illustrated," and works of literature of varying lengths are accordingly wittily transformed by this pictorial way of serving up the written word. Long short stories are especially suited to the form, and among those I began to consider as material for me to adapt were Noël's own.

Knowing his severe disappointment with other people's adaptations of his works, especially in their Hollywood incarnations, I was more than reluctant to propose myself for a task at which others had failed. There was always the question of writing dialogue for his characters where none was provided in the narratives, and of adopting his own personal, highly individual style with words. I could almost hear him explaining that no American could reasonably be expected to write convincing dialogue for, say, the Cockney charlady in *Mrs. Capper's Birthday* or for any number of other inventions of his in stories I thought cried out to be dramatized. He would add that if he were to undertake writing a woman from Brooklyn his ear would inevitably fail him. He said just that, in fact, when the matter was finally suggested by me, but he later reconsidered and gave his full permission to go ahead.

Yet beforehand I experimented a little, having a handy source of reference in the notebooks I had kept throughout the years. When I began looking at them I found one that appears to have been reassembled at some point in the interests of unity, marked with connective squiggles that are meant to set a time and a place for each entry. The unity I was searching for may have had something to do with an essay I thought of writing for a magazine. Noël had once identified himself to me as "one of the few remaining guardians of the English language," and all these notes concern, in one way or another, his love for words and the surprising ways he found to use them which made so much of what he said vivid and memorable.

Living in London also made clear to me what I had only dimly comprehended earlier, that Noël's trusteeship of spoken English had a far greater significance than I could have suspected. In England, the misuse of a single word may in polite society reveal all, shatter a carefully developed disguise of refinement and the best schooling, expose a vulgarian in the mask of a gentleman. "Lounge," for instance, as applied to a private sittingroom, confirms a suspicion that the speaker is attempting to conceal his working-class origins, and establishes his insecurity in elevated circumstances. "Dentifrice" is another dead give-away.

Noël took a great interest in the controversy occasioned by the publication, twenty years ago, of Nancy Mitford's personal view of the English language, which gave currency in England to the terms "U" and "Non-U" as a means of differentiating blood-lines through certain usages. He called it a "drizzle in a teacup." The battle raged chiefly in the letters-to-the-editors pages of the posh Sunday newspapers, where "lounge" was as fiercely defended as Agincourt ever was.

A part of the dispute focused on the polite name for the paper on which a bread-and-butter letter was written; it was held by some to be "letter paper" and by others, whom Miss Mitford identified as not belonging to the upper class, as "note paper." The American "stationery" was shunned by both factions. "Lavatory paper," to identify a domestic necessity, was roundly denounced as a genteelism, "toilet paper" was unacceptably Yankee in origin, and only "loo paper" passed muster in Miss Mitford's book. The latter gave rise to much conjecture with respect to the etymology of "loo" (one explanation was fetched very far to connect "water closet" with "Waterloo"), and how to refer in an elegant and well-bred fashion to the once unmentionable feature of household plumbing so occupied the columns of *The Times* of London that the newspaper called a halt: "This correspondence must now be terminated" wrote a full stop to the whole affair.

"Sad news, I'm afraid," said Noël. "Now we shall never know what *Times* readers think is meant by the everyday word 'wife.' "

A don at one of the provincial English universities (Non-U) had suggested that "wife" was the most ambiguous of all words in English, its precise meaning altered by the pedigree of the speaker and his social footing with the husband of the wife named. If the wife of the former made reference to the wife of the latter, excepting she be a blood relative, without identifying her by name ("Remember me to your wife" rather than "Remember me to Jane"), she was guilty of (a) openly insulting the man by insinuating that his spouse was not of gentle birth; (b) saying that she did not know the man well enough to pretend to a familiarity with his wife's first name and, moreover, was content to let things remain that way; or (c) pretending to an intimacy with the man that others within her hearing could not have previously suspected or later verified.

Unassailable gentlefolk, or so the argument ran, avoided "wife" altogether and so, evidently, had a much easier time of it. But there were pitfalls here, too, as when a marchioness or other titled lady, saying good-bye to an untitled man named Smith, added, "And do say hello to Mrs. Smith, won't you?" leaving Smith to wonder if he was meant to greet his wife, as was his custom anyway, or one other of the Mrs. Smiths of his aquaintance and, in the latter case, which one?

It was this part of the confusion that gave Noël so much pleasure. He said he had toyed for a long time with the idea of writing a revue sketch or even a song dealing with the many risks of social embarrassment inherent in the use of the word "wife," but abandoned the notion for the reason that, among the members of the audience, too many innocent minds would be troubled by memories of past lapses when they had unwittingly used the suspect monosyllable.

"I kept picturing poor, dear Nancy Mitford as a house guest at some baronial estate, in Wiltshire or Norfolk, having been shown all the blue-ribbon cattle and praising them later to her hostess, unable to use the taboo word 'cow' for fear of causing offense and opting instead for 'the bulls and their wives.' "

The self-styled "guardian of the English language" was not a purist, however. He loved the vernacular and, after testing it for a time, would seize upon a new expression and use it repeatedly if it seemed to him an improvement on the accepted way of saying a thing. He first heard the term "beatnik" at Las Vegas and thought it was a legitimate Yiddish word, but once it was explained to him that it came from beat music, the word instantly became his own and was rarely employed without a modifier: a "beatnik" was often "devout" and, at least once, a note I made records, was "as yet unconfirmed." I was often amused at how vintage slang endured in his conversation. "Nuts" continued to mean "crazy" to him long after it had been discarded by everyone else. "Nifty" was employed to diminish objects of importance whose value was implicit in their names: Josef Hoffman had played on a "nifty Bechstein" and a London producer flashed "a nifty Fabergé cigarette case". In England, the word "tatty" signifies anything derelict or shopworn, and Noel made of it a *mot juste* by applying it to the Palazzo Vendramin in Venice and the Orangerie at Versailles. To be "with it" came as a novelty to him and caused him to remark that he had never been "without it"; accordingly, the expression was used in his own personal understanding of it: J. Paul Getty and Queen Elizabeth were "with it," but others of more modest means were not.

Sir Michael Redgrave, who also has a way of treasuring the English language as if it had been developed for his exclusive use, entertains the theory that Noël took pains to invent a special English for himself, one that would permit of all kinds of foreign intrusions and modish expressions to spice up a sentence and give it his own personal style.

Sir Michael recounts once having heard Noël describe a hotel in the north of Italy and its staff: "I dread the look of that dwarf *cameriera* with the obviously damaged tear duct who brings me that sinister breakfast each morning five minutes too early; she makes my eyes water *en sympathie* and I'm very nearly *bawling* by the time she withdraws."

"I suppose," adds Sir Michael, "it's the experience of having written all those lyrics. The sentence I quoted has a kind of scansion with a distinct rhythm but no rhyme. However, it contains an Italian noun; an expression used by French doctors; a very old-fashioned bit of American slang; and ends with an unexpected verb in the German style. And I do *not* think Noël ever said anything that had been prearranged in his head; it was instinctive with him, and just naturally flowed out that way."

The visible badges of respectability and affluence were often deflated with adjectives generally employed for quite different things; thus, so-and-so had "only a *modest* Renoir and a *tiny*

Winterhalter portrait of her grandmother" and someone else had an "inconspicuous Rolls-Royce she had specially designed to look secondhand." Yet some struggling actors in Greenwich Village lived in "an impressive duplex they insist on calling a 'cold-water flat'," and a beach hut at Quogue was an impecunious writer's "splendid seaside residence." A famous formal garden in Surrey looked "quite untended and lifeless," and one of the royal country retreats was "a nice weekend place if you know how to fish."

"Everything smells like something else," Simon remarks to Victoria in *Shadow Play* after she has said that lotuses smell of pineapple; "it's so dreadfully confusing," and to Noël each of the senses was receptive of comparisons. The lobby of the St. Regis Hotel in New York smelled to him uncomfortably like the piano department at Harrod's, and a dish of flaming bananas made him think of nail-polish remover. The sky over the Thames had a Venetian look, not a clouded one; the Strand in a rainstorm was as wet as Singapore on a festive occasion; and the Midland Hotel in Manchester was a provincial touring company of the Paris Ritz.

In America all sirloin steaks looked like bedroom slippers to him, and if the film showing at the old Roxy movie palace was no good, one could always look away and pretend one was rather drunk in the post office at Granada. Las Vegas was a luxury cruise liner so vast that one could not see the ocean from it, and Beverly Hills looked like an uncommonly bad Raoul Dufy. Filtered cigarettes tasted like Kleenex, and the sofa in a London screening room had been upholstered by a compulsive manicurist with her discarded emery boards.

Strangers on the street or at restaurant tables were studied carefully to determine exactly whose twins they were. If the resemblance was only partial, or limited to a single feature, it was seen to have been an exchange of some kind: "That waiter has wickedly

stolen Lilli Palmer's nose," or "Whatever can have possessed poor
Margaret Rutherford to lend her chin to the Princess Murat? I must
ask her."

If certain faces always "dimly," "faintly," or "almost" called
other faces to mind, at least two of them were stubbornly regarded
as belonging to one person. During the latter years of World War II
a pair of Hollywood blondes were pushed to stardom despite their
similarity of appearance. Noël said he was certain that they were
one and the same girl taking advantage of the acute labor shortage,
and had anyone evidence that they had ever been seen in public
together? Finally the blondes appeared as sisters in a cotton-candy
Technicolor musical comedy in which their likeness was more
emphatic than ever before. "Remarkable," said Noël; "she has
discovered the split-screen technique which used to be the exclusive property of Boris Karloff. Do you suppose she gets a double
salary for this?"

Faces were also understood to be in a transitory state and
frequently seemed to be in a dreadful rush to look like someone
else or to be marking time until the right original came along who
might be copied. When Truman Capote's first novel, *Other Voices,
Other Rooms,* appeared, it wore a dust jacket with a photograph
of the author reclining on a Victorian settee with a wistful stare into
the camera. "What will this face be like twenty years from now?"
Noël wanted to know. "At the moment it isn't so much a *face* as
a pre-face."

Buildings and monuments looked like inanimate objects (the
Pavilion at Brighton was "nothing but a lot of pepper-mills") and
sometimes people did, too ("Edith Sitwell, in that great Risor-
gimento cape of hers, looks as if she were covering a teapot or a
telephone"). A couple he met in the Orient were misshapen, the
husband enormously tall and seemingly tapering upwards to a

point, the wife less than average height and global in appearance. "I thought," said Noël, "when they stood side by side, that they must still be advertising the 1939 New York World's Fair." A woman once mistook him for Rex Harrison. He asked her, haughtily, "Do I look as if I sold Bentleys in Great Portland Street?"

Performers, even in repose, were sometimes described as movements: when Betsy von Furstenburg made a memorable New York debut in a play of Philip Barry's, Noël thought her "the subtle gesture that can silence an unruly mob," and of a Hollywood columnist notorious for fawning on those she admired, he said, "I see her as one great stampede of lips directed at the nearest derriere."

So much of what Noël said was seized upon by the press that reporters invariably lay in wait for him at steamship arrival points or plane terminals, their notebooks at the ready, hoping for an exclusive quip, and he rarely disappointed them. On these occasions, brushing through a swarm of them in a V.I.P. airport lounge, one word would often suffice. "Mr. Coward, have you nothing to say to the *Sun?*" a lady journalist once asked him. "Shine," he said pleasantly.

"That soon became a device," he recalled, "and I had a stock of imperatives to offer practically every newspaper published in English. They always put the question that way: 'Have you something to say to *The Times?*' I always say very gravely, 'Change.' But being expected to say something devastatingly funny becomes very wearing after a while, and if you happen to come up with something not absolutely first-rate it is agony to see it in print.

"There was a time, many years ago, when I was very fond of finding new varieties of the wages of sin. I went about saying that the wages of sin was this, that, or the other—indigestion, or boredom, or success, or something. I got very tired of that, but for years

144

thereafter I would find these 'wages of sin' remarks quoted in print as shining examples of my 'wit' and I would cringe and blush and make embarrassed noises every time I saw one.

"I do not think I *am* particularly witty, though I am often capable of making people laugh uproariously and continually when I am feeling at the top of my form. And I enjoy that enormously. But wit—true wit—is social criticism, and its object is to *deflate.* Wilde's line about the woman whose hair had turned quite gold from grief is pure wit. Familiar though it may be, it is funny to this day. It is not a cliché because it is still true to this day. The line of mine that is, I suppose, the most frequently quoted is, 'Women should be struck regularly, like gongs,' and it is called 'witty' but I don't think it is. It is funny—or was—because of the hostility in it and because of the surprise of the word 'gongs' which is totally unexpected in the context. The line says nothing that is true, whereas Wilde's woman's hair speaks volumes about everything from widowhood and sentiment to vanity and inheritances, and works on several levels all at once.

"I believe one of the great secrets of making people laugh is to surprise them, and one of the surefire ways to surprise them is to use a non sequitur or a name or idea totally out of context. I said once, and with a perfectly straight face, something perfectly sensible and, for me, perfectly true. I said that Celia Johnson could become one of the world's greatest actresses if she didn't keep having babies all the time. This was received with such gales of laughter and was quoted in the press, and I am unable to see anything funny in it at all. It is a statement of my sincere belief that Celia's domesticity is more important to her than is her theatrical vocation."

Once, on a visit to Beverly Hills, friends had taken him to a nightclub where the entertainment was the kind of attraction that was considered the ultimate in "camp" among the bores and bored of the Hollywood culture desert. The performer was a giant of a black man, possibly with antecedents from the Watusi tribe in East Africa, and he was very thin. He danced a kind of ceremonial ritual, wearing only a loincloth that was described as having been something more than explicit. His body had been dusted with asbestos powder, and at the climax of the dance he set himself alight, flames seeming to leap up from every portion of his lanky body, until the loincloth was a cinder and what remained of it dropped to the floor.

On the evening Noël witnessed this doubtful divertissement, the fiery dancer came so near to his table that he shrank back in feigned alarm.

"Is there no *limit,*" he cried, "to the talents of Peter Ustinov!"

The element of surprise, the introduction of a word or name in a context where it did not belong, and the sudden, unrelated predicate were the staples of Noël's technique for making people laugh. This technique only gained in effect by his habit of snapping out the quip so rapidly that a great part of the surprise originated in the speed of its delivery. When repeating a favorite remark that Noël had made, his friends regularly follow it with a snapping of the fingers, say, "Like that," and express astonishment that there had been time to think of the words themselves.

In London I came to know a number of people who knew or had known Noël very well. All of them shared a love for him that was touched with more than a little reverence. All of them had lovely stories to tell, of some surprising act of kindness that was not uncharacteristic but nevertheless a surprise, of telling bits of direction he had given them as actresses, of a few "words to the wise" that had counted for so much at an unhappy time. Most of them had treasured anecdotes that, for one reason or another having to do with delicacy, resist publication and survive today only when a gathering of the clan takes place, the clan who feel his loss less severely when they are able to bring him so amusingly to life with their memories.

In the capacious anthology of stories about Noël and what he said in a given circumstance, certain examples have become so classic that they are ascribed to other, lesser wits. The most enduring of these has been, at one time or another, attributed to such divers worthies as Tallulah Bankhead, Mae West and H. L. Mencken: Noël's famous postcard from the Louvre. On the back of a museum photograph of the Venus de Milo, Noël had written to a friend, "You see what will happen if you keep biting your nails!"

Much of what Noël said does not survive a voyage westward. His view of a production of *Macbeth,* in which Sir Alec Guinness had Simone Signoret, speaking English on a stage for the first time, as his Lady, was dismissed by Noël as *"Aimez-vous* Glamis?" a delicious pun that in order to raise a laugh needs a familiarity with how Shakespearean place names are traditionally pronounced by English actors (in this case, "Glahms"). Certain of the sharper things he has had to say in America, by the same token, do not cross the Atlantic in the opposite direction, as when he went to the opening night of *The Wisteria Trees,* a misguided transplantation of Chekhov's *The Cherry Orchard* to Louisiana, and said he felt he had spent "A Month in the Wrong Country."

Those who have a reputation for being good company and for making people laugh with a few correctly chosen words at the right moment, for introducing a seeming non sequitur at a moment when a sequitur would have fallen appallingly flat, know that no conscious effort is required. A verbal facility born of years of experience as a storyteller, or merely a weekend guest, is only a part of it. Women, generally, are better at it than men. Freud examined both wit and laughter in a noble and solemn way that did justice to his learning and his interest in everything that makes men *feel;* it was a pioneer attempt, if somewhat parochial in that his examples were understandably those of a Viennese who had little time to go about socially, and at a period when the jokes were not always good. His conclusions were that "wit"—an ambiguous German word that comes into the English language through his translators—had only one source, and that a subterranean one: people laughed because of a communion of hostility towards a given object between the speaker and the listener. Many samples of wit—in the sense that Freud examined it—illustrate this analysis, but Noël's view of it was, if anything, deeper than the psychoanalytical one.

"People will often protect themselves by laughing, it is quite true," he once said when we had begun to generalize about comedy, and why things were funny to some people and not to others, "and what is funny is often that which we pray can never happen to us. The most simple-minded illustration is the banana skin. And yet even the banana skin can fall flatter than the man who steps on it if it isn't *timed* properly. I wish Dr. Freud had studied the subject of timing. It might have proved most helpful."

The clipped and staccato delivery combined with the polished vocal tone and impeccable timing of each word gave to Noël's remarks the fillip that elevated them to the status of wit. Because they were of the fleeting moment and came so nimbly to the tongue, his remarks often do not survive transfer to the printed page without a lengthy preamble, and even then lose much by being read rather than heard. If his wit was evanescent, he himself sometimes thought it worthy of repetition. At these times there were always a few prefatory words, like "Have you not heard what

I said recently about that?'' or "Do you not know what I call it?'' or even, though rarely, "Let me tell you what I said the other evening that amused me as much as it did my dinner guests.''

In any lengthy disquisition on a given subject, such as the reticence of the English, the food in American restaurants, or the curious inability of an actress's wig to imitate real hair, he employed a surprising alteration of speeds to give pace to his speech and make sure that it was not interrupted. Favorite words repeatedly turned up in these discourses, with an exaggerated stress ("dis-*gusss*-ting"; "monu*men*tally tiresome"; *such* a waste of time") and the letter "r" could be trilled or rolled out the length of a rataplan for emphasis. He was able to use alliteration in conversation without ever sounding affected. Once, at a summer luncheon, the fruit was praised: "Really remarkable raspberries, these." One had to acknowledge that they were exceptionally good as well as that he had found the only possible way to describe them.

His habit of seasoning much of what he had to say with interjections or beginning a sentence with little overtures ("Nowadays, however," or "I used to think," or even "by and large") created in some people the impression that, like Maugham, he had a slight stammer.

Michael Redgrave disagrees. "It wasn't a stammer. No word was ever interrupted and no syllables repeated in the middle or anything of the sort. I think his head worked so rapidly that he frequently had the impression he had already said something when he hadn't. He'd merely thought it. And then he would have to take stock of what had been omitted, and pause to get it right, and come in with one of his 'on the wholes,' or shake his head and say, 'dear boy.' "

Many parlor mimics attempted impersonations of him and few

succeeded, but Daniel Massey, who is Noël's godson, was well known for his superb Coward impression long before he was chosen to play his godfather as a young man in the film *Star,* a kind of fantasy-biography of Gertrude Lawrence.

Noël had been hearing for years about Massey's accurate takeoff of him without ever having heard it himself. Having retained the option of approval of the actor who was to play him in the film, Noël agreed at once to Massey, provided the young actor perform his impersonation for him. The audition took the form of a conversation which Noel later said was exactly like talking to "a mirror with a memory" and found somewhat unsettling. Massey asked him if he had any criticisms.

Noël reflected for a moment. "One," he said. "Too many 'dear boys,' dear boy."

"The 'dear boys' or 'darling girls,' " Redgrave observed, "were merely Noël's way of catching his breath unnoticeably, as we all have to do on the stage when we have a long speech or a difficult mouthful to say. And even though there were a good many of them, the 'dear boys' and so on, they were always, *always,* unerringly placed."

He paused, though not for breath.

"But then," he added, drawing on his pipe, "one could really say that about him geographically, and also in *time. Noël* was unerringly placed."

10

Throughout 1964 I divided my time about equally between London and places on the Continent: the little hill town of Asolo, an hour's drive from Venice, where the Brownings had lived and Duse and d'Annunzio had found peace; Barcelona, in the middle of a frigid winter; rural Greece and the island of Rhodes, scorched by desert winds blown northward from Africa. An American editor persuaded me to write travel essays for his magazine, and I found they were astonishingly easy to do if they were scrupulously researched; I was unable to understand a new place and write about it with honesty unless I immersed myself in its history and got to know some of its people. Travel, in the fifth decade of my life, provided an education both sentimental and disorganized at the same time as it enriched my purse.

In the autumn of that year the National Theatre of Great Britain added a revival of Noël's *Hay Fever* to its repertory, the first living dramatist to be so honored, and invited him to direct it. I finally decided to abandon my diffidence in the matter of asking his permission to adapt his fiction, wrote to him at some length and was given the green light by return mail. Negotiations between his agents and the television company, normally a lengthy process, were conducted swiftly, and Noël retained the privilege of approval of the scripts as well as veto in the matter of casting the leading roles. I completed three adaptations in record time, sent them off to him, and flew to Naples on a writing assignment. I spent five weeks of a semitropical winter there, and it was with delight that I learned Noël wasn't very far away.

It was his sixty-fifth birthday, and he had fled to the island of Capri to escape the noise and festivities that would have been certain to erupt had he remained in London for the occasion. Yet his whereabouts did not go unpublicized, and the little post office in the main piazzetta was awash with hundreds of cablegrams and greeting cards for him. The early morning boat from Naples carried a floral cargo of birthday offerings along with a few dispirited Caprese returning from the mainland and myself, bidden to come to lunch.

December 16 that year was a warm and humid day on Capri, yet Noël wore an emerald-green ski cap and a heavy Norwegian fishermen's sweater with a turtleneck when we met on the terrace of a café in the piazzetta. He sipped an Americano and ripped open a batch of wires signed Ruth and Garson and Binkie and Alfred and Lynnie and one from the Queen Mother and another sent by all the waiters of the Caprice Restaurant in London, which seemed to please him the most.

"You haven't thought to mention my cap," Noël said. I started to say something in praise of it, and nearly said it, when he raised his hand in a familiar gesture that called for silence. "No, no no, you don't like it, and it doesn't matter, nobody does. But I look less like a mandarin in it. I shall probably wear it always."

In fact, he looked more like a mandarin than ever before. There was, in certain lights, and when seen from certain angles, a distinctly Oriental cast to his features, an aspect that the passing years tended to exaggerate. He had always made fun of this, as if by pointing out his resemblance to a Chinese ceremonial portrait painted on silk, or a music-hall poster advertising the newest magician from Peking, he made it unnecessary for others to note the likeness. Osbert Lancaster did a masterful caricature of him in kimono and queue, but I thought it made him look like a fatigued Samurai after a hard day's work rather than an aristocrat of the Celestial Empire. That morning he gazed out at the movement to and from the post office and up and down the steps to the vegetable market, as a detached observer remarking every detail. He might well have been a visitor from the Far East.

The piazzetta, with its three cafés, five entrances, church and campanile, always resembles the setting for an operetta, even in winter, but with the summertime people absent the life of the community, the daily business of keeping the place going, is more noticeable, and Noël gave it his full attention. His eyes followed the movement of the delivery barrows piled high with winter cabbages, the passage of a swarm of blue-smocked orphans en route to morning prayers, the efforts of a telephone linesman to settle the foot of a ladder securely on the uneven stones of the pavement. An expensively dressed woman with a café-au-lait complexion and two elderly Bedlingtons on a tandem lead crossed in front of the café on her way to the post office.

"I haven't set foot on Capri for decades, but that same woman is still here and doesn't seem to have changed a bit. Can it be the climate?"

"She has a house in the Via Castello," I said. "Some of the foreigners stay on all winter—Gracie Fields, for instance. And I suppose the little Arab with all the rings does, too."

"*Which* little Arab with all the rings?"

As the devil is said always to appear at the merest mention of him, the diminutive, wizened Arab emerged from the post office with a package in hand, his garnet-colored fez tilted forward on his brow, his tentlike apparel moving pendulum fashion over his orthopedic footwear as he approached what he thought were two potential customers for the shoddy rings he was wearing. He murmured something, but an imperious gesture from Noël waved him away. He backed off in the direction of the funicular entrance as if withdrawing from a royal presence.

"He has," Noël said, "a faint look of Beatrice Lillie about him."

Soon there was an invasion of dogs in the square, about a dozen of them, of all near-pedigrees and shapes and sizes. A Christmas tree lay on its side on the steps leading up to the church, and the dogs found it an engaging lavatory before hurrying off elsewhere in their mad pursuit. Two remained behind, however: a brazen, tawny Golden Retriever of dubious pedigree having an olfactory flirtation with a not-quite-good-enough Blue Collie.

"Have you ever noticed," I asked, "that all the dogs on Capri appear to have had one distinguished ancestor from abroad?"

"Exactly like the natives," said Noël.

He remarked on the sameness of the place, on its seeming

unwillingness to pull itself out of the 1930's for the accommodation of its contemporary visitors; everywhere one looked there was some detail, some feature that was indelibly stamped with the taste of the earlier decade. The bathrooms at the Quisisana Hotel had water faucets and other articles of plumbing so like the fixtures of an equivalent *hôtel de luxe* in London that it was clear the English milords who once helped turn Capri into an international playground had been consulted about their installation. Noël was often amused by the Englishness of far-flung places, the kind of sub-colonialism expressed by the appearance of a tea cozy on a sun-baked terrace at Taormina or the Cockney slang of a pair of chattering mynah birds in a bar on Mallorca. He himself almost rigidly left his Englishness behind when he traveled, embracing each introduction to local food and drink or novel custom with relish and good grace.

He had read some of my travel essays in magazines and said he thought they ought to be collected into a book. The same idea had occurred to me, but I couldn't think of a theme that unified them sufficiently, and he shot me a look of impatience. "Travel itself! *Travel* unifies them! Rose Macauley said that travel is the *subject* of the life of the civilized human being!"

There was very clearly something unspoken in the air, something he was planning to say to me that day that I knew I would hear before I embarked for Naples again, and I wondered if it would be a new topic rather than the old and familiar "urbanity" lecture, for which my recent life had now equipped me with a number of pungent answers. But, as always with Noël, his route to the subject was circuitous. For a time I thought it would concern the television adaptations, but it soon developed that he was planning to read them while on Capri and that I would have to wait before hearing what he thought of them. Perhaps, visiting Capri after not having seen it for several decades, and having commenced his sixty-sixth year that morning, he wanted to talk about what he wanted to see again in the world before he was too old to revisit the favorite haunts of his young manhood. I was partly right, but there was something much deeper, which was to remain unspoken that day, as if he had just begun a kind of summing-up of the past and had not fully come to terms with the contradictions he found in it.

"I have always wanted to write a travel book," he said, "and perhaps I shall one day. But the book would be like no other, in that it would not dwell on the beauties of Angkor Wat or what the Taj Mahal looks like by moonlight, and it wouldn't contain facts about the horses of San Marco in Venice and how Napoleon transferred them to the Carousel arch in Paris, or any of that. Rose Macauley did all that anyway.

"No, my travel book would be a highly personal one and nonetheless instructive for that. It would contain passages about the pancakes with maple syrup that used to be served at Child's in Columbus Circle at four o'clock in the morning, and the teams of dray horses that once would pull the brewery wagons up Ebury Street when I lived there. And it would certainly record my enduring puzzlement over that clock in the tower there with its pretty chime and its secret knowledge of what time it really is. I have been sitting here for three successive mornings now and my bewilderment increases by the minute. I thought at first that the chime was not synchronized with the hands and that it was warning one what time it was going to be four minutes hence. I now conclude that the chime *is* in fact a warning, but an ambiguous one, and tells you that in four minutes' time it may be four o'clock, or three, or perhaps even two. I find it is quite charming.

"I don't suppose one could do a travel book solely in terms

of the hotels one has stayed in throughout the world, yet the odd thing is that my memory identifies a place by the kind of accommodation offered there, and my experiences of the sights and monuments and so on seem secondary to me, finally. The Acropolis is magnificent, of course, yet once seen and examined, it is never again going to come up with a surprise. On the other hand, the hillside below it with its little tavernas and open-air dining places and crooked streets fills me with the pleasure of anticipating the unexpected, which, as often as not, takes the guise of chance encounters or a mournful tune played on a distant flute. Those things make me very happy indeed. Let's go and have lunch!''

It is generally tacitly understood that one cannot eat well on Capri, yet Noël insisted he had made an arrangement with the proprietor of a rather plebeian restaurant near the port to prepare certain Italian specialties better known to the farmhouse kitchens of Piedmonte than to the expensive eating establishments recommended by Michelin in their *Guide to Italy*. He had ordered, for lunch, a traditional Italian winter dish: lentils cooked with spinach, carrots, onions and garlic, served with a brace of sweet and pungent sausages in a large soup bowl. He hoped I would like it, and I said I knew I would..

We descended to the port via the funicular and walked slowly together to the somewhat unpromising restaurant. A baker's dozen of tables, covered with checkered cloths that were damp but by no means fresh, stretched across an expanse of unwashed glass that had ambitions to becoming a picture window. Outside, the sky was pewter; the bay of Capri had the artificial look of a marine landscape.

"Good God!" said Noël, on hearing a pair of mandolins playing "Arrivederci Roma" as we entered. "Strolling musicians! They weren't here yesterday."

The chairs were not comfortable. The cutlery was stained with detergent spots. The wineglasses wanted a good polishing and the wine itself had a doubtful history, yet Noël was able to beam at the whole display as if he were seated in the garden restaurant of the Ritz in Paris. "It's such a pleasure to be somewhere *else* for one's birthday," he remarked to the bay. He tasted the ersatz wine.

" 'Rough,' some people might say. I think I'd call it *brutal*.

"You're going to be in Paris in January? What do you plan to see?"

I said I had always wanted to see Mme. Edwige Feuillère as *La Dame aux camellias*, and that she was going to play a season of it once more at the Théâtre de l'Atelier. I had been looking forward to it for so long.

"I'm afraid you'll be bitterly disappointed," he said.

"Oh, I can't believe that," I said. "It's supposed to be on a par with Laurette Taylor in *The Glass Menagerie*."

"Rubbish. Do you not know what I call it, her much over-praised performance?"

"Tell me."

"Camille faut."

Noël attended to the cleanliness of the rim of his cloudy wineglass with the tip of his right index finger. When I had stopped laughing I opened a little notebook and wrote down the double entendre. He elevated his eyebrows slightly. "For your memoirs?"

"Something like that," I said.

"I once took Vivien Leigh to see the legendary Camille of Madame Feuillère, and I swear that the curtain had not been up for five minutes before dear Vivien was awash in tears. I was so astonished that I simply struck her rather sharply on the wrist and said, 'Stop that!' Whereupon she did. Always obedient, Vivien. I mean, the first act of that play is in fact rather gay, with only a hint here and there of the doom that is to follow, long time in coming though it may be. But Vivien had been brainwashed, you see, by the excessive praise accorded Madame Feuillère by a certain English critic who thinks anything in French is bound to be superior to what is written in his native tongue. And I simply wouldn't have it! I sincerely think one must always distrust legends, particularly French ones. But do go and see for yourself."

I closed the notebook and put it away in my pocket as his eyes followed the movement. "That will appear in print one day and merely perpetuate my reputation for being a prime bitch. I don't really care. But it would be nice if sometimes the *kind* things I say were considered worthy of quotation. It isn't difficult, you know, to be witty or amusing when one has something to say that is destructive, but damned hard to be clever and quotable when you are singing someone's praises!"

He stared at a little steamer on the horizon making its daily journey to Sorrento. "I wonder if I *should* write a travel book or not. I know that my body has wandered a great deal, but I have the uneasy feeling that my mind hasn't kept up with it. I worry a little about my mind, you know.

"By and large, it is a good mind, well trained and disciplined and able to record impressions and retain them easily and sort things out into their proper relationship, one with another, and maintain a sense of proportion without much effort, and so on. I can make rapid and logical decisions which later turn out to have been the correct ones. I am a good observer, particularly of microscopic details. Had I been a painter I should certainly have been a miniaturist. My mind functions best when I am dealing with people, and it is at its worst when there is some abstraction to worry about.

"I am very good with faces, such as that woman's in the

piazzetta this morning. And I can recall to mind a melody I heard in an obscure revue forty years ago as if I had been whistling it incessantly ever since. But my mind's eye does not, for instance, retain a landscape, or the shape of a woman's hat, as Proust's could, and yet my powers of memory in all other respects are very strong.

"I have read eclectically but there is a whole body of literature that means nothing to me because it does not give me pleasure, and great quantities of recorded human experience that hold no interest for me whatever. In fact, my mind resents certain kinds of information. The fact that a certain beautiful church is notable because it is constructed of some kind of stone being used in ecclesiastical architecture for the first time interests me not at all. I just like the look of the church.

"Antiquities frequently irritate me. The Coliseum stands there, you know, suffering from too many centuries of appreciation. The seven wonders of the world have a way of looking smug and grand at the same time, simply because it is expected of them.

"And yet I love the whole business of traveling, some place new, some place old, it doesn't matter. I like the incessant movement of getting to where I'm going. At these times I function best, I write best, I compose best. Just to be off somewhere seems to bring out the best in me, I don't know why.

"There was quite an irritating little piece about me in one of the Sunday supplements not long ago that concluded mistakenly that I have no interest whatsoever in the structure of society, in politics, or in contemporary morality, which is quite absurd. The author drew these conclusions from a reading of my plays—at least, I assume he did. It is quite true that, for the most part, my plays deal with the customary and accepted topics of whatever particular genre they happen to belong to. The comedies are invariably about adultery or the course of true love, running rough or smooth, and the melodramas and pageants deal with stiff-upper-lip patriotism, all traditionally tried and true subjects and audience-pleasers, I am happy to say. Had I written a play about, say, the two gentlemen from the Foreign Office who defected to Russia and took some secrets with them, and the misgivings they felt later, not one critic would have sat still for it, and very few members of the audience, if they had bothered to come at all.

"I am personally very much interested in what is going on in the world today, in the power struggle and the disruptive elements that make all society at every level seem to be standing on shifting sands. I don't write about it, that's all. I don't know that I should be very good at it, and certainly the audience and critics wouldn't think I was."

It was impossible to interrupt one of his monologues once he had got started, much as one would have liked to ask a question or pursue a particular viewpoint further, and they would end as abruptly as they began, with a little gesture of some sort, as if to say, "That concludes the lesson for today."

The lentils arrived and Noël sniffed the aroma approvingly; as if summoned by a theatrical callboy, the "strolling musicians" arrived as well.

They beamed, and Noël thought to remove his cap, and beamed back at them, his fork poised above the lentils. He murmured some appropriate welcome to them in Italian, and added apprehensively to me in English that they were probably going to play one of his songs. I said I thought that unlikely, but sure enough, although not surely enough, the two ham-handed Caprese strummed away at their mandolins, producing a tune that sounded only vaguely like "I'll See You Again."

"I cannot *bear,*" said Noël, settling his fork into his untasted plate of sausages and lentils, "to hear my own music badly played! And how ever could they have known that I wrote that?"

He rose slowly from the table and reached out for one of the mandolins, taking it from the man nearest him. "I don't imagine they can read music, but neither can I. They must have picked it up off the radio."

He began to pick at the strings of the little instrument, one by one, and achieved a kind of *pizzicato* effect of the famous song. I said it was the first time I had ever heard it played *that* way, and he acknowledged that it was a novelty for him as well. "But I haven't had one of these things in my hands for decades."

The second musician played a kind of accompaniment as Noël instructed the first one in the proper fingering of the strings, finally restoring the mandolin to the man's eager hands with a benign smile. Resuming his seat at the table, Noel waited an agonizing few minutes, barely concealing his distress, while the mandolinists struggled through a passable rendition of the tune. At last it was over, and the instrumentalists backed away from the table with the most courtly bows they could manage.

"I'm so happy they didn't call me Signor Romberg—they often do," he said, digging his fork into the sausage at last. A grimace followed. "Stone cold!"

He called for the plate to be removed and ordered some local cheese and an apple. The talk turned to my television dramatizations. He wondered if they had taken very long to do.

"Pretty Polly," I said, "took me only seven days." I regretted the remark the minute I heard myself say it.

He pursed his lips in that cryptic way that I always construed to be expressive of disapproval. *"I wrote Private Lives in a week-end."*

"I heard that years ago, but I never knew whether to believe it or not."

"In the Cathay Hotel in Shanghai, and with a very bad cold."

After the apple and cheese there was a good round of hand-shaking and some faulty English as the waiters and the management tried to express their gratitude for his fidelity to the restaurant, and then we were outside on the *quai* once more. He was unsteady on his feet even then, before the circulatory illness that later so debilitated him was detected, and he held on to my elbow as we moved along the promontory that led to the embarkation point of the returning boat to Naples.

The winter sun disappears behind the peak of Anacapri surprisingly early, and the landing stage was discolored with a purple light. "A rather Oriental light," said Noël. "You've never been to the East, have you, dear boy?"

I said I hadn't, but that I meant to go.

"Yes, and the sooner the better, because it is changing rapidly. No man can call himself truly educated without having spent at least a year out there. I may go again myself quite soon."

It was time for the little steamer to return to Naples. "Come back next Tuesday for lunch. It will be better then, I promise."

"What can I bring you?" I asked. "English newspapers? Luigi Barzini's *The Italians?*" I stepped onto the narrow gangway.

"No, no, don't bring me anything. Just your love, but I see I already have that."

He gave a little wave. "Oh," he added, "and, of course, your notebook."

11

The following Tuesday the sea was choppy, and a dull gray mist obscured Anacapri from view like a lady wearing a hat with heavy veils. Noël had taken up his position on the café terrace, dressed exactly as I had seen him last, and was fretting over a difficult crossword puzzle.

"Order yourself a drink," he said, "and help me out with this one. I think they have got a new man to set the puzzles in the *Telegraph;* this one is bloody difficult."

I ordered an Americano, while he gazed thoughtfully at the capricious clock. "Eight letters for the first word, five for the second. Together they mean 'The state of mind producing the remark,

"We are not amused" '—and I cannot make an anagram out of any of it, so it must be a pun."

He put the newspaper aside and resumed a pair of knitted gloves. "I had no idea," he said, "that television writing was a technique all its own. It is more continuous with theatre writing, is it not, than with writing for movies?"

British television had not, in those days, adapted to the use of film or to color. Plays were acted consecutively and recorded on tape; only in extraordinary circumstances were these tapes interrupted, and only if no solution could be found in the writing to obviate the interruption. I explained this to him.

"Yes, I see that you are obliged to reorganize the narrative in some instances to accommodate an actress making a costume change and the like. And you have done it very skillfully, and there are little added scenes that do not come from my story but aid the telling of it considerably. Very deft."

I told him about the aesthetic of television as it was understood by the English, that it was "radio illustrated," that the *word* was its subject and that the visual shenanigans beloved by American television directors were considered by their English counterparts as representative of a total misunderstanding of the medium.

"I have been taught something," he said, with a grateful nod. "I have observed, when watching the lesser screen, as I call it, that what is offered up by the BBC is so much more commanding of the attention than American television, but I thought it was the absence of commercials and nothing more. In the cinema, of course, the pictorial is paramount, even at MGM, and the word is secondary, which it took me some time to learn.

"When I started to write *In Which We Serve* I plunged into it as if a film were perfectly continuous with the technique of writing for the theatre, except that the individual scenes were

noticeably shorter. I was blissfully unaware of the enormous differ-
ences between the cinematic way of telling a story and the theatrical way. I did not know that one could begin a scene in the very
middle of it, without gradual preparation and building up to its
climax. I did not know, for example, that one might have a shot
in the ward room of the destroyer between two officers without
having to show one of the officers making an entrance into the
scene. Nor had I any notion whatsoever of the technique of 'mon-
tage,' by which great periods of time and numerous events of the
deepest significance could be shown meaningfully by means of a
rapid series of different shots. I was in a state of happy ignorance
about all of it, which my first draft clearly revealed to David Lean
and Ronnie Neame.

"However, I learned rapidly, and I now know a great deal
more than I did—principally, I think, that films are really made in
the cutting and editing and not in the writing of them on so many
reams of paper. I don't think I should ever want to write anything
again directly for the screen. I am an uneasy collaborator, and the
camera is so omniscient and powerful an ally that I confess that to
try to think as it does makes me somewhat nervous. You cannot
say to a camera, 'Now, do you see it this way, as I do?' because
it may see it exactly the other way and yet cannot reply that it does.

"Ronnie Neame spoke for his camera so well, and David Lean
for the movement and placement of the actors so brilliantly, that
I do think the screenplay I finally wrote is fully cinematic and a very
respectable achievement.

"What we had to cope with to get the film made at all during
wartime is so wearying to recall that I have managed to suppress
a good deal of it in my memory. But the Ministry of Information
came into the picture when the head of its film department wrote
to the Lords of the Admiralty to say that he had read the final script

and found it to be exceedingly bad propaganda for the Navy, as it showed one of His Majesty's destroyers being sunk during enemy action, and that in no way could the producers hope to receive permission for the film to be shown outside of England so long as the hostilities continued. This information terrified everyone connected with the production, and it looked as if the whole project would have to be abandoned, at an enormous financial loss, a few weeks before we were to go before the cameras at Denham Studios. But Dickie Mountbatten came to the rescue, and the letter-writer was personally dressed down by him in such a way, in my presence, that we had no further interference from the Ministry of Information.

"The British film industry is notoriously inefficient, extravagant and wasteful, even to this day, and I had been warned on all sides that it was a hotbed of intrigue and treacherous unpleasantness. None of this was ever visible throughout the long weeks of shooting *In Which We Serve,* for our crew were entirely different, cooperative and seemingly inspired by the story to do their level best, much as the gallant seamen did in the story itself.

"I have seen the film on numerous occasions throughout the ensuing years and I am still, I'm happy to say, very much pleased with my own performance in it, though how it came to pass continues to puzzle me. I was then, and I still am, made very irritable by the necessity of saying the same few lines over and over again while the camera photographs me in long shots, medium shots and full close-ups, practically invading my mouth or my nostrils with the microphone dangling somewhere overhead. To this day I do not see how some of the superb acting performances I have witnessed in films have ever been achieved by this method of repetition. However, I am astonishingly good in the movie.

"By the time I came to do *Our Man in Havana* for Carol Reed,

I was used to the process and didn't grumble about it so much. Carol would film me in a brief shot, saying some quite ordinary line like, 'Pass the mustard,' and then say, 'Cut,' and say, 'That was absolutely marvelous, Noël; only *you* could do it that way. Now let's do it again, shall we?' and I would do it again and try to be even more absolutely marvelous than I had been in the previous shot, and this was just a bit of foolery on Carol's part and we both knew it was, but it worked quite well and I wasn't the least bit fractious during the making of that picture, or don't think I was. Did you see it? I thought I was awfully good."

The clock in the tower chimed once. We looked up to see that its hands pointed to three minutes before twelve. "Now," said Noël, "we shall see what time it thinks it is."

We waited patiently. The single chime, as he had determined from his observation the previous week, was a warning that the hour would be announced in a matter of minutes. I ordered another drink while we waited, and recalled our first meeting in Connecticut long ago when the firehouse siren had sounded to signal the end of the workweek and he had reacted with such astonishment. The piazzetta was empty and oddly silent, the stones of its pavement glistening with wet.

From the archway to our left there emerged a sudden apparition, three male figures who might have stepped out of a sylvan scene painted during the Renaissance: small, sturdy men in chestnut-brown leather knickers, sheepskin capes and tricornes, and heavy homespun stockings. Slung over their shoulders were sets of musical pipes with a bellows attachment like some primitive version of the bagpipe.

"Good heavens!" exclaimed Noël. "The Italian Tourist Commission really goes too far!"

Had I not seen the men in Naples a few days earlier and had

them identified for me I should have been equally surprised. They were shepherds, acting out a centuries-old custom of the Christmas season, who came down from the hills as troubadors to beg for alms. In some mysterious way the Italian faithful regarded this annual visit as connected with the Nativity, the winter solstice, and as a harbinger of springtime as well, and even the poorest among them did not refuse the shepherds a few lire when their tricornes were held out to them in the classic gesture of beggars. I shared this newest bit of useless information with Noël and he nodded appreciatively.

"I was so afraid they were going to play 'I'll See You Again,' " he said.

We fished some coins out of our pockets and dropped them into the hat of their leader, and the trio chorused their thanks in a dialect that was strange to the ear. They shuffled across the wet stones and disappeared through a different archway, in the direction of the Via Castello.

"They'll show up at St. Peter's in Rome for Christmas Eve mass," I said.

"You have become very Europeanized, dear boy," he said, examining me studiously as if to identify the outward signs of this transformation. "Do you know it?"

"In what way does it show?"

"In an attitude of mind. To me a cultivated mind is above all an inquisitive one, restlessly curious about everything. I can think of any number of clever people with costly educations behind them who would have regarded those shepherds as picturesque and amusing and never thought to inquire about the wherefore of them."

"And is that only a European thing?"

"It is most noticeable in American expatriates, let's say. Europe comes as a great revelation to clever Americans from which they never quite recover.

"Look at it! Today that silly clock has refused to acknowledge noontime. Think of all the poor dear *signore* in their clockless houses on the hillside below waiting to know when to put the pot of water on to boil for the day's pasta and the chimes don't sound. Their husbands come home from their labors starving for nourishment and the pot isn't even on the boil. Think of the drama!"

"I wonder," I said, "if that is the explanation for the fact that every garden in Capri has a sun dial."

"An unreliable timepiece at best, and today especially. I hope Coley and Graham weren't listening for the stroke of noon. But their appetites will soon tell them it's getting on for lunch time. I don't know *why* that clock confounds me so much, but it does."

He lit a cigarette and resumed his scrutiny of the crossword puzzle then. He filled it in from the bottom squares upwards, still struggling with the elusive answer of an eight-letter word and a five-letter one that would reveal the unamused state of mind. I was then unfamiliar with the elliptical trickery of English crossword puzzlers and could solve only those where the definitions patently suggested an anagram. Many writers and composers are puzzle addicts, but Noël's concentration on the pattern of black and white squares he held before him was of an intensity that seemed to me out of all proportion to the kind of pleasure he could possibly derive from it, and somehow unreasonable. I never saw him at work, or at the piano when he was composing, but I felt that I was seeing him as he was when the juices of creativity were flowing and he was exercising his imagination freely. He gave a little gurgle of pleasure and filled in the topmost squares.

"Got it?" I asked.

"Victoria Cross," he announced in one of his ringing theatrical tones. "I ought to have got it at once."

Graham Payn and Cole Lesley, dressed for an English December or a winter race meeting, shuffled into the piazzetta with sleepy looks. They thought we should all move into the café's interior, the oddly humid day was not one to be spent in the out-of-doors; it was the kind of ambiguous weather that invariably brought on aches and pains or nasty chills, and the "Master" knew it full well.

It was the first time I had heard him so designated by anyone, although it became general to refer to him as the "Master" in his later years even in the press, and I gave a little confused smile when I heard it. As Coley used it, it took on a mock-servile coloration, as in Edwardian novels of genteel households where butlers and housemaids employed it deferentially; it also made Noël sound officious and demanding. Much later I came to understand the degree of affection, and the respect, the term expressed, but for the moment its novelty troubled me. The Master preferred to remain where he was, and wanted another drink, and thought that there was no call to descend to the port for lunch via the funicular: the little restaurant behind the church knew its business as well as any other on the island—which was, of course, saying very little.

The details of travel arrangements were examined, Coley placing a special stress on booking rooms at the Excelsior in Rome for one night as a safeguard against there being a wildcat strike of the airlines, always a possibility in Italy. Had a car and chauffeur been arranged to meet them in Naples and drive them to Rome? It had been, at least a month before. It would be prudent to confirm by telephone that the car would, in fact, be there.

Having recently experienced numerous frustrations and

delays in getting from one place to another on the Continent due to the suddenness of my decision to spend the holidays in Italy, I was filled with admiration for the efficiency with which the travel arrangements for Coward and Company were ordered. They all seemed to know precisely where they were going to be the penultimate Friday in February, what time would be best to board a liner sailing for the Seychelles Islands early in January, with whom they would dine and where on the fifteenth of next March. That Coley was superb at keeping facts and figures of this kind in his head so that he might produce them at a moment's notice was abundantly clear, as was his loving consideration for everything having to do with the Master's comfort, appetite and health. Having begun his association with Noël as a manservant and developed by degrees into his secretary and, later, companion, he was better equipped than anyone to function on each of these levels. Moreover, there was never a sense of duty or strain in his performance; neither was the familiar and slightly superior air of the paid companion ever evident. He was a loving caretaker proud of his charge.

As we sat there on the terrace, all eyes fixed on the clock in wait for its next caprice, I realized it was the passage of time and the fact of physical deterioration that cried out for expression in the semitropical damp. Noël's movements were perceptibly far slower than they had been the week before, and a certain spirited bounce was absent from his manner, though the rapidity of speech and the astonishing quickness of his mind was in no way impaired. True, Noël was entering a new cycle of his career: *Hay Fever* at the National Theatre was the outstanding success of that season and the one that followed, and he said he was busily at work on the third volume of his autobiography. But I knew that that undertaking required as little of his energies as the writing of a half-dozen letters every morning. I had not heard him mention any work-in-progress, only projected revivals, and I was overcome with an ineffable sadness.

The restaurant had few customers other than ourselves when we entered, and the selection of the right table accordingly was a matter for serious consideration. Coley investigated suspected draughts; Graham found the noonday glare in a bright corner too strong for him; Noel wanted to see the port while he ate. A compromise was achieved: we sat out on a kind of sun porch that was both airless and shadowed yet commanded a belvedere of water and the sloping purple cliffside, extravagant with terraced orchards. Noël expressed his delight at having Capri practically to ourselves; the absence of tourists was understandable, but the Caprese themselves had evidently gone into hiding, for even the boatmen were missing from the *quai*. I said it was another of those surprise religious holidays in which the Italian calendar abounds, and this initiated an informed discussion, partly resulting from a careful reading of Luigi Barzini's witty and instructive history of the Italian people, of the national character in all its variants from one end of the peninsula to the other. Ancient words going back all the way to the vulgate were redefined: I said that *subito* did not mean "immediately," but "in about twenty minutes," and Noël, welcoming the idea of an improved dictionary, offered *magari,* a common expression meant to reassure the hearer that what is hoped for will soon come to pass, as meaning "never," or "not a chance." It was a variation of a popular game of a decade earlier called "Fractured French." The game, requiring nimble mental calisthenics, was played throughout the meal and accompanied by so much hilarity that the *padrone* and his wife would peer around the curtains separating the restaurant proper from the sun porch to make sure that it was not the cuisine that was funny. The food was indifferent, but Noël had managed to charm two bottles of French burgundy onto the table after numerous insistences by the management that only local wine was available. My curious request for a tall glass filled with ice and a small pot of espresso to pour into it bemused the waiters for a time, but when it arrived Noël decided he would like the same thing and we drank delicious iced coffee with our cheese and fruit.

The shadow of Anacapri darkened the island and it was time for me to go. Noël and I walked to the funicular landing and he said that it would be some time before we saw each other again but to have no qualms about my television adaptations. His only admonition was to be scrupulous about the choice of actors and to be on my guard for "Americanisms" in the dialogue.

I looked at him fondly, with a smile for his green knit cap tilted absurdly forward on his brow, and we shook hands.

" 'Partir, c'est mourir un peu,' " he quoted. "A sentiment Cole Porter so deftly plagiarized."

"Like many before him," I said.

"Well, I suppose, really, it must have been Ulysses who said it first. Take care, dear boy." He gave his little wave and I stepped into the cab of the funicular.

Waiting on the *quai* below to board the ferry, I heard the demented clock chime four; transmitted by a watery breeze down the cliffside, it sounded like a distant, passing bell.

12

Throughout the succeeding winter and again for a period during the autumn of the next year, I worked on further adaptations of Noël's stories. An adapter has a specific responsibility to the original material he is making into a play, and when a deep personal loyalty to the author of that material is involved, the task is one of scrupulous watchfulness that nothing of the adapter's individual style intrudes upon the finished product. With certain of the stories, my job was easy: their narrative structure was such that they could be lifted scene for scene from the printed page and reassembled in script form with a minimum of additional material or exposition. Others presented problems of reorganization, of compression, of altering a time sequence, of eliminating characters who served only to provide color and amusement and had no dramatic function. With these I felt I needed Noël's counsel every step of the way; if not his specific solution for the difficulty, at least an acknowledgment that one existed and that he had no objection to drastic measures, surgery or the introduction of foreign material.

But he had fallen ill in the Seychelles Islands, had been flown to Rome to a clinic, and was recuperating only very slowly in Switzerland. A long letter I sent received a cable in reply, that he "was trying to rise above it," and from it I knew that I would be proceeding on my own with only my instincts and best intentions to guide me. It seemed a good plan to read through as many of his plays as would be helpful; if I could immerse myself so deeply in his style and manner and his approach to dialogue, I might learn something of his technical facility that would give to my own material a coherence with his, like invisible weaving or the final moments of the opera *Turandot,* left incomplete at Puccini's death and finished by another composer.

Accordingly I read everything I could lay my hands on again and again; the ease and the inevitability of the writing, the surface polish, the deceptive simplicity of execution at first defied rational analysis, but I persevered. My admiration, always great, for Noël's comedies was only enhanced by dissecting them; I examined them with a microscopic interest, laughed a lot, and learned a good deal. At a point during the last act of *Easy Virtue* (written in 1924) it becomes evident that the insupportable stuffiness of her husband's family has been the cause of the failure of the heroine's marriage. It is not the first liaison she has been obliged to terminate by the act of packing up her things and walking out; there were others before, of an ambiguous nature, and she has been divorced at least once. A sympathetic male friend asks her what she plans to do and where she means to go.

"The Ritz," the lady says. "I always do."

It was one of Coward's favorite lines. It is illustrative of his particularly oblique method of delineating character through the irrelevant and unexpected and his economy of language in shaping a line which, in the hands of an accomplished actress, will produce the desired laugh. But the scene containing this line is a dramatic one: the woman is seriously disappointed and even saddened at the way things have worked out for her; there is nothing for her to do but make a splendid exit on her marriage with as much dignity and even nobility as she can muster; the friend's question is prompted by a sincere concern for her welfare. Once the question has been asked, she might reasonably reply that her intention is to go to London to see her lawyers, to try to organize some kind of orderly future for herself, to spend some time alone to reflect on where she has gone wrong. Yet her need to put a good face on things, to stiffen her upper lip and preserve her self-esteem as a very modern woman of the world, is stronger than the sentiments she feels. "To the Ritz," by itself, might serve as a serious answer, accompanied by a sigh, or a certain tension of the hands. But, no, she is in a play by Noël Coward. She must be impaled like the butterfly she is, and so "I always do" is the inevitable accompaniment to naming the hotel, and everything that we know about her from what has gone before is perfectly crystallized in the one brief speech.

Nor will any hotel other than the Ritz serve Coward's purpose. That bastion of respectability and foreign Royalties, Claridge's, would be the wrong choice; a married woman unaccompanied by her husband would not stay there for a prolonged visit. The Savoy had, in those days, a somewhat "fast" reputation with theatrical guests and noisy late-night parties in the Grill, and Brown's would have been full of the kind of stuffy, conservative people she was fleeing from. The Ritz, with its cachet of unassailable dignity, its connotations of the good life enjoyed at fantastic prices, and its aura of romance and even intrigue, was the only *right* place for the Coward heroine, in her circumstances, to stay. Had she been going to Rome rather than London, Coward would have booked her into the Grand.

"Any writer worth his salt is only naturally compulsive about details of that kind," he had said once when we were talking about his fondness for Proust's work and the fact that Proust had once risked a massive attack of asthma by leaving his cork-lined room to go and inquire of a celebrated beauty who lived in the country exactly what kind of hat she had worn to a party years earlier. "Proust was perhaps an extreme example of the artist who wants to get every detail *right,* but to my way of thinking it's only part and parcel of the *job.* People constantly tell me about Oscar Hammerstein's search for months for a three-syllable word that would establish exactly how high the corn was in 'Oh, What a Beautiful Morning' and one is expected to be amazed at his dedication, whereas I am not. The word 'elephant' was *there* all the time, inevitable and waiting for him to come upon it. He might as easily have found it in an hour, but he didn't. That it took him three months until he was satisfied is merely a fact of life of the artist's daily *job.* And don't ever forget it!"

"You seem to be happily free of stresses like that, though," I said.

"I write very rapidly, you mean? Yes, I feel that if it takes a long time to do it, and it gives me trouble to do, then there has been something fundamentally wrong with it from the outset. This does not hold true for everyone. But I must please myself. *I* must like it. I have never had to search for elephants for three months, but

I have spent very uncomfortable weekends looking for a good rhyme for Balenciaga."

I looked a question. "Forsyte Saga," he said.

Alan Brien, when he was critic of the London *Sunday Telegraph,* pointed out that the texts of Coward's plays and musicals throughout the years were studded with geographical references, more of them, he thought, than in the work of any modern playwright. It puzzled him that a man of such worldliness could hope to produce laughter in the theatre by merely mentioning suburban towns like Surbiton or remarking that the county of Norfolk was very flat. Fixed in print, these place names seem to have no comic intention; their service appears to be to set a character in his environment and class origins if his accent has not already succeeded in doing that. But in the theatre the names of places ring out like the whir of an arrow on its way to the bull's-eye and produce the shock of recognition that evokes laughter.

In *Relative Values* (written in 1951) the Countess of Marshwood's lady's maid is, after many years in her service, giving sudden notice of her intention to quit that very afternoon. Her reason is that an uncle has died and that she must go to care for her bedridden aunt who has no one else to look after her. Something about this story does not sound quite credible to the Countess, who questions every detail of it. Where exactly does the invalid aunt live? There is a pause, while the lady's maid invents a suitably distant locale. After a time she settles on Southsea. How did the uncle die so very unexpectedly? The invention falters again for a moment, and then the news is supplied: he was run down by an Army truck and killed instantly. Where exactly? The answer comes in a great rush: "Just opposite the South Parade pier, my Lady."

In the written text, this series of interchanges between the servant and her mistress seems to be nothing more than a device to reveal to the audience that something has gone wrong, that the maid is giving her notice for a reason too difficult or too embarrassing for her to explain, which, in fact, is the burden of the plot. A first-act curtain is about to fall in a minute, and the speech that brings it down is a simple statement of fact containing a very carefully prepared surprise. But the play is a light comedy, not a melodrama, and the questions-and-answers preceding the curtain are written in brisk, short speeches, a few words at a time, in a time-honored technique of scene construction whose purpose is to create a sense of speed.

In performance, the pause preceding the naming of Southsea as the residence of the fictional aunt produced the expectation of something inappropriate to come, and Southsea did not disappoint; the laugh that greeted it was followed by a bigger one as the Countess pursed her lips and lowered her eyes in an eloquent expression of distaste and disbelief. One need never have visited Southsea to appreciate the horror of it as Dame Gladys Cooper, playing the Countess, remembered its unsightliness and tried to banish its memory forever. Every member of the audience had a fleeting mental image of the working-class seaside resort; it needed only the mention of the South Parade pier, so carefully placed in the sequence of dialogue, so absurdly and impertinently *out* of place in a manor-house library, so obscenely on the lips of a servant seeming to be ungrateful to her titled mistress, for laughter to explode from the audience in great shouts of delight; on a good night the laugh was accompanied by applause.

There is a term employed in the theatre for this kind of measured comedy writing: "character comedy"; it defies analysis if it does not defy description. Noël himself was often reluctant to talk about the mechanics of producing laughter, saying that in the writing of a funny scene he never was certain that something was "right" but was always uneasy when he felt the necessity to tinker with a series of lines, changing the order of words or slashing a line from a manuscript one day only to restore it the next, in which case it invariably turned out to be "wrong." As laughter is more easily suppressed in the theatre than it is generated, fastidious practition- ers of comedy, actors and authors alike, tend to worry about it: even a sure-fire joke, a "snapper," a line of dialogue that has had a gratifying response for a hundred performances, albeit to a vary- ing degree, may unexpectedly be greeted with a deafening silence at the hundred-and-first. If this fault is maintained for three or four performances successively a polite form of panic results, and every possible object of blame is examined: the weather (a rainy night often produces a damp and uncomfortable audience; a hot one is notoriously stunning to the spectators' attentiveness); another actor has made a novel and distracting movement so that the funny line was not heard; the lighting is different and so the speaker cannot be seen clearly and as a consequence the line cannot be heard. The anthology of apology for purloined laughter is already copious, but new excuses will be thought of to explain it away until the day when comedy exists no more.

"During the run of *Relative Values,*" Noël had told me, "Gladys Cooper said that Angela Baddeley, who played Moxie the housemaid, was losing both her laughs on the Southsea lines, which seemed to me very strange indeed. I didn't think it was possible, unless Angela was doing too much with them, as was entirely probable—telegraphing them or playing them straight out front. Anyway, I thought I'd have a look and went round to the theatre one night during the first act to see what was going wrong. I couldn't see anything wrong at all. It wasn't a rainy night.

The lights were as they had always been. Everything was the same.

"But the theatre was as silent as Lenin's tomb for that scene, and Gladys said it had been that way for about a week, so it was quite obvious that something very different was taking place on-stage and I wondered what. I went back the next night and it was the same thing all over again. There *was* one slight difference, so slight that one would not even think of remarking it. Gladys, seated in a wing chair, with Angela standing to the left of her, was sitting a little farther into the chair than she had been directed to do, a matter of a few inches, no more. This repositioning was very nearly unnoticeable, even to me, but what it had done fascinated me. In order for Angela to look directly into Gladys's face when she said 'Southsea' and the line about the pier, she had had to turn her head ever so slightly upstage, without realizing it. No more than a fraction of an inch.

"I didn't speak to Angela about it at all. I merely told Gladys to try sitting forward again a little, as she had done at the beginning, and she willingly obliged. Accordingly, Angela looked again directly into Gladys's face and, accordingly, the laughs returned as mysteriously as they had disappeared. Perhaps even a bit bigger than before, now that I think of it."

"Is that *instinct?*" I asked. "Can that be *learned,* or does one only know it by instinct?"

"A combination of instinct and experience. I can give an actor a direction I *know* is right, but if I am asked to explain my reason for doing so, I am at a complete loss. You will hear in some quarters that I am 'infallible' in these matters, which is nonsense. I have been wrong. Not often, but I have been wrong."

The legend of Noël's "infallibility" was particularly wide-spread in London, and at the time I worked on adapting his story

"Pretty Polly," Lynn Redgrave, who played the title role in the television play, provided a fine example of it. As a member of the National Theatre company at the time, she was playing in *Hay Fever* at night while rehearsing in the television studio by day. I asked her what it was like being directed by the "Master."

"Well, I've never felt before or since," she said, "that I was completely putty in anyone's hands, but with Noël you simply do what he tells you like an obedient child. The first day of rehearsals I was terrified. I think we all were. The experience of being directed by the Master is not one that has been shared by very many of my contemporaries. I was word-perfect, of course, as we all were, except for Edith Evans. The character I play is a mindless, quite silly debutante called Jackie, and I had this notion that it would be funny if she lisped. The word 'appendicitis' occurs several times in my lines, and I thought it would sound funny with a 'th' substituted for every sibilant, so I learned the part that way. At the first read-through, Noël sat out front with Olivier and listened to the whole thing approvingly until at one point he leaned over to Sir Laurence and said, in the most penetrating stage whisper I ever heard, 'Does the Redgrave child have a speech impediment?'

"I was convinced he didn't like me, and that perhaps I had been forced on him in some way through the National's policy of role distribution, but he never gave me notes or specific instructions or anything and he never mentioned the lisp, except to say, '*Lithp* clearly and beautifully, dear,' which I thought I had been doing all the time. And then one day it became shockingly evident that the third act of *Hay Fever* was only fifteen minutes long and would have to be stretched to a half hour, with each one of us making our contributions to padding it out. My assignment was to invent lots of 'business' as I came down the stairs to breakfast at the beginning of the act. So I descended the stairs very slowly, a step at a time, talking to myself *sotto voce* in a kind of lisping baby-talk. And at each step I would pause, as if a new thought had just occurred to me which I would have to discuss with myself.

"This seemed to work quite well, and sent the others into gales of laughter, and I was quite pleased with my inventiveness. Until one day not long before the opening in Manchester, I got my first note. Noël told me to go directly over to the sideboard when I finished coming down the steps, to stare at the breakfast on display there, then suddenly turn away, cover my eyes with my hands, and burst into tears.

"I demanded to know why. Noël said he had once seen Marie Lohr do exactly that in some play long ago and that it had been hilarious. I said it didn't sound hilarious to me at all. But he was insistent. Not only was he insistent, he gave me a specific count of one-two-three. One, look at the sideboard; two, turn away and cover your eyes with your hands; three, burst into tears. I had never acted on the count of one-two-three before, and said so. And I was told to please just do it *his* way and no other and not to ask questions. It was hilarious and he had no idea *why,* but it would work.

"Now, I suppose you've heard about Noël's infallibility, and that the better part of wisdom is to follow his instructions to the letter, that he is always right. Well, this is the test of that legend, I thought. And of course the business got the most enormous laugh on opening night in Manchester and ever after. Here in London, I would sometimes consciously vary the timing, pausing between the one and the two, and the three, just to see what difference it would make. And the difference was that the laugh would be rather feeble, like a laugh that wanted to explode but couldn't. I am not one of those intellectual, examine-every-little-thing actresses, but I finally concluded that my breaking into tears had been carefully prepared for in the writing by the other characters' dismay at the quality of the food they were eating that particular weekend. Witness Maggie Smith's big laugh on the line, 'This haddock is disgusting.' It has all been neatly established by the others, and *I* reap the rewards. But the count of one-two-three is something I shall never understand."

"And," I said, "it always works?"

"Always. I don't examine it, I just do it. I suppose that's what comes of having a long memory along with sound theatrical instinct."

Miss Redgrave confirmed one of the most persistent anecdotes concerning the Master's difficulties with Dame Edith Evans during the *Hay Fever* rehearsals. Dame Edith had the line, "On a clear day you can see Marlowe," referring to the view from her garden, and rendered it repeatedly as "On a *very* clear day you can see Marlowe." Noël corrected her every time she introduced the extra word. Finally, when the word 'very' had come into it once too often for him, Noël said, "No, Edith. 'On a clear day you can see Marlowe.' On a *very* clear day you can see Marlowe and Beaumont and Fletcher!"

It was another instance of the inappropriate place name in an ordinary context that provoked laughter, laughter he knew would not come if two extra syllables were added to the line. When Alan Brien's complaint about Coward's use of place names was published, the Master said, "It hadn't occurred to me that I rely heavily on the names of places for comedy, and yet I suppose I do. There is something irrationally but intrinsically funny to me in the name 'Slough' whenever a railway station announcer says it, and there always will be. But places and the names of them have also a distinct feeling for me, so that in my story, 'Mrs. Capper's Birthday,' the young couple met at a picnic on Box Hill. It was wartime, and

Londoners didn't travel terribly far afield for their outings, yet when Beryl Reid said in the television play that she had met her husband at Box Hill, it was funny. I have no explanation for that at all. There is actually nothing funny at all about Box Hill. I remember it as being rather somber."

Most writers of comedy emphasize the necessity of placing the strong word, the operative one that provokes laughter, at the very end of the line, and practitioners of stand-up comedy, such as Jack Benny, are adamant about it, working and reworking their jokes until the right word to be stressed has been found, through trial and error, and securely placed at the end to trigger the response. (A good illustration would be Benny's classic: "I've been in London four days and already I've spent seven pounds. Next time I'll come *alone*.")

But Noël was unwilling to accept this dogma as Holy Writ and felt that an actor's ability to "gabble" a speech rapidly in a cascade of language could produce a comic effect independently of the positioning of words. What concerned him greatly, however, was the circumstance of a single speech containing two laughs, one at the beginning or in the middle and a second at the end. "The first laugh," he said, "is secondary in importance, and the danger is that the actor will lose the more important one by getting the first. There are audiences who will laugh at everything, and when you have one of those you must seize control of them and allow them to laugh only when you want them to. Otherwise your performance is a shambles. Learning how to suppress laughter comes only with long experience, but it is essential for a comic actor if he wishes to continue in his profession. When one of those laugh-happy audiences comes along, and they occur much more frequently than you would think, you must do far, far less, almost nothing, reducing every customary emphasis to the merest stress, and all

186

kinds of things to slow down the pace imperceptibly, letting the story and situation carry you. Because they will laugh anyway, you see, and for too long, and your timing suffers. It is all terribly confusing when it happens.''

In *Nude with Violin* a jolly, plump ex-chorus girl called Cherry-May Waterton has called on the wife of a recently deceased artist with the news that she had once been the man's mistress and has a letter from him guaranteeing her a certain claim on his considerable estate. She has brought with her a muscular young Frenchman, Patrice, who speaks no English and, in fact, has no dialogue at all in the play. The wife receives her cordially and manages, with some effort, to overlook the woman's cheerful vulgarity and the crudeness of her speech. In a long and meticulously written scene, Cherry-May recounts the history of her stormy relations with the deceased, punctuating it with a number of expressions, such as "bloody," that cause the wife to wince, and excusing herself for each indelicacy with the words, "Pardon my French." That Patrice may be kept *au courant* of all that is being said, Cherry-May translates into execrable French many of her crisper lines and even some of her fatuous ones, and words like *"dépasser"* and *"bienvenue,"* spoken with the accents of East London, tumble out of her with a fluency and speed that is eccentric and hilarious while the lines are in no way amusing in themselves. Courtesy compels her then to explain to the wife what she has been saying to Patrice: "I was just telling him that we mustn't overstay our bloody welcome, pardon my French."

Taking Cherry-May's courteous tone, the wife replies, "I don't understand French," and the mad, irrelevant reply, the inane response to the apology for "bloody," misunderstood to mean an expression of regret for using a foreign language in the presence of someone who so clearly does not understand it, added to the statement of a plain fact that has been more than clear to everyone, touches off the kind of laughter that, in the theatre, frequently develops into applause. It is a particularly good illustration of Coward's comedy technique, the almost careless insinuation of the genteelism, "Pardon my French," to excuse gutter English, the speed of the horrid French translations to distract the audience, and the carefully prepared confusion in the wife's mind of which language is meant when the word "French" is used. A scene structured as neatly as that is the result of experience and skill, certainly, but without the sure instinct of the theatrician for what is and what is not funny it would never have been written at all.

"Certain words are funny, to me. I don't know if it's the sound of them merely," Noël said, "or some bizarre picture they conjure up in the mind's eye. What is funny to me is not necessarily funny to anyone else, and one always has to give something a trial. The word 'blancmange' to describe an especially odious pudding is funny to me because it is so thoroughly ludicrous to call a glutinous mass of tapioca or whatever, something that should never be seen outside of the nursery, by a French name that means 'white-eat.' The etymology of the name doesn't interest me at all; it is simply one more example of the inappropriate and, hence, to me, comic. Many years ago in a revue called *Words and Music* I wrote a line for Beatrice Lillie describing a woman as 'a blancmange with a henna rinse' which was received with a notable lack of amusement by the audience. I changed it to a 'blancmange in a reddish wig' and that didn't work, either. I reflected that perhaps a mass of hair on top of a pudding made the image even more disgusting than the pudding itself was, and very nearly abandoned the notion entirely. Then I thought I would have one more go at it. The woman referred to in the sketch wore a shapeless afternoon dress pinched in at her very rotund waistline. The line was changed to 'a blancmange with a sash,' and had a very satisfying response indeed. There is no explaining it.

"In an earlier revue there was a sketch I stubbornly held on to for a time before throwing it out completely because it was, in the main, not funny. It had a line about the Prince Regent, later George IV, and it had amused me when I wrote it and I didn't understand why it didn't amuse the audience. The line was, 'Of George IV there is absolutely nothing to be said,' which is utter nonsense, as there is a great deal more to be said about him, of a delightfully racy nature, than there is about any dozen of the monarchs who preceded him. I tried every conceivable way of saying it, always with the identical results. I gave it a leer. I tried it in a very aloof, foppish way. Always, the same stony silence. One night I expanded the line. 'Of George IV there is absolutely nothing to be said,' and paused, and added in a sort of stricken voice, 'except that there is nothing to be said.' It was greeted with a shout of laughter, as it was at every performance thereafter until I threw the sketch out of the show.

"One can examine that until one has turned mauve with exhaustion and never find a satisfactory explanation for it, and I wonder that it is worth the bother, really. One can become much too self-conscious about comedy and literally worry it right out of existence with too much analysis. Only when something is a proven laugh and suddenly it isn't any longer, *that* is when to examine it scrupulously and try to see what has gone wrong. Oh, it is so eminently *worth* it when the laugh comes back."

There were unforeseen difficulties in adapting "Star Quality," the longest and most ambitious of his stories. His other fiction reveals strong influences: tropical environments, mayhem among the mangroves, and large quantities of steaming rainfall are the trappings of Maugham, and the Promenade des Anglais in the days when that was an exact description of the thoroughfare and not of a boardwalk belongs to the world of Colette. "Star Quality" reveals no influences other than Coward's own brilliance, and in it more is to be learned about the man than can be found elsewhere in his writings. Of nearly novella length, it is written with an icy, controlled rage that dictates every scene, tracing the agony of a fledgling playwright's initial professional experience in the world of the theatre from the day he first meets the actress who will make his sentimental drama a success until the opening night in the West End of London.

A knotty problem presented itself here: the published story omitted a key scene between the hero and the young girl who loved him; it was referred to somewhat obliquely in the text, made its narrative point, and was forgotten. Dramatically the play needed the scene; without it the hero lost a certain sympathy and conviction. Moreover, it required a certain length, and time for the audience to appreciate the sincerity of the girl and to understand why she was being so uncompromising. I searched about in the story like a scavenger, trying to find words of Coward's that could be given to the two characters and furnish out the scene with them, but there was nothing suitable. The question of how Noël would have written the scene, where he would have placed it, what attack he would have taken to keep it light and amusing and in keeping with the manner of the body of the story, was one I could not answer for longer than I care to remember.

One day, seated at the typewriter and staring at the blank sheet of foolscap in its carriage, I allowed my mind to wander back over my meetings with the Master, recalling conversations we had about his early days as a struggling young dramatist.

"I was totally indifferent to everything in life that did not take place on a stage," he had said, and I had admitted to a similar obsession. "All the frustrations and cruel disappointments were, I always knew, eminently worth it, because one day they would pass and I would succeed. With only a few shillings in my pockets, I would spend one of them on a sticky bun and a cup of tea at a Lyons Corner House and queue up for the unreserved gallery seats with the rest to see Dame Marie Tempest in some trifling vehicle and, oh, it was so very much worth going hungry just to watch her. I knew that if ever I should have grandchildren I should be able to say to them, 'When I was young, I saw Dame Marie Tempest!' Although now the truth of the matter would be that I could say, 'When I was young I wrote plays that Dame Marie Tempest *acted* in!' "

Setting down his recollections as though they were those of the young playwright he had written about in language that was characteristic of the boy and the period of the play seemed a good idea; the scene—to borrow a familiar author's statement that has more bravado than truth in it—practically wrote itself. I simply sat the boy and his fiancée down in a London espresso parlor and let them talk. The experience of spirit-writing has been described by aficionados of the occult, and it would be fanciful to ascribe the finished scene to some wandering disembodiment of Noël dictating it over my shoulder, but a more scientific explanation that a psychoanalyst might offer would probably be nearer the truth. In any event, the scene as written, and later performed without changes, is pure Coward.

Because of its length and the difficulties of casting the leading roles the dramatization did not reach the production stage until nearly two years after it was written. The Master, with a retinue of friends, saw it at a private screening in London at the producing company's building in Hanover Square. Irene Worth sat at his left, I at his right, making myself as small as possible in my chair when the interpolated scene commenced on the small screen. For his memories of Dame Marie Tempest I had substituted similar ones of Dame Edith Evans for the character of the young playwright. When the actor who played him reached the line, "When I was fifteen years old I spent the last of my pocket money to see Dame Edith Evans from the gallery," Noël said very quietly in the darkness, "I hope she remembered her lines."

I shrank farther into my chair as the scene progressed, knowing that the whole thing had been a mistake, that the story could as easily have done without it, that my invention was no match for his and that the interpolation stood out as an intrusion upon the material as Noël had originally conceived it. He saw it through before turning to me to say, "That scene isn't in the original story, is it?"

I swallowed hard. "We all felt it was needed."

"Quite right," he said, and returned his attention to the play.

The character of Lorraine, the actress with "star quality," is the most richly rounded woman Coward ever wrote. She is coy and flirtatious and tough as nails, worried about her age, stupid about everything outside the theatre, determined that everything that is done onstage shall be according to her dictates, and a lovely, sometimes endearing, woman of a vivid and ripe sexuality. Her vanities and excesses remind some people of Gertrude Lawrence, although Noël himself insisted she was an "amalgam." He hammers away at her relentlessly and exposes every one of her nerve ends, concluding with admiration for her and, in so doing, spells out his own ambivalent feelings for the world of the theatre, its glories and its miseries, its truth and its sham.

The story is in no way ambiguous. If Coward sees Lorraine as a monster, he also sees that she is a very sacred one indeed. Her quality as a star transcends all human error. She is a fine actress and there are too few of her breed about. The theatre needs her. The young playwright needs her, for without her his play would never have reached the stage. The young man will learn from her, will learn much about his craft, and in future will write plays that do not need "star quality" as insurance at the box office. He will also learn how to use his experience of her when future temperamental wars of nerves are waged. It is all in the order of things, Coward says, horrid and demeaning and senseless things, but unavoidable and sometimes even fulfilling.

Late in the play the actress reviles the director for his lack of understanding, for his inability to cope with her mercurial personality, for his slandering her behind her back, his roughshod treatment of her at the expense of the play and, by extension, of the young author. It is a scene of calculated complexity: the actress is screaming from the bottom of a well of fear, is only dimly conscious of the import of what she is saying; her stated aim is to see that a great personal friend of hers, a mediocre actress, is not to lose the secondary role Lorraine had fought so hard to have her play. In this objective she is totally foolish: her friend is harmful to the play and woefully miscast. It is unlikely that the woman could find employment elsewhere. Yet it is not the loyalty of great affection that underlines Lorraine's passionate defense of her friend: as Coward has merely suggested in the story, the star needs a loyal companion at her side, to have lunch with, or send out for coffee, to spy for her on the enemy camp and to tattle tales. But, in the hysteria of her tantrum, the greater part of what Lorraine says when she abuses the director is objectively *true* and makes perfect theatrical sense. As Glynis Johns, with her customary insight, played this scene, exposing every uncertainty that motivated the explosion while continuing with her self-righteous attack on the hapless director and touching at her hair as though an insect had flown into it, the agony of the woman's situation became more than Irene Worth could endure. She wept. Noël looked away from the screen at her.

"I don't understand why you're crying," he said softly.

"No," said Miss Worth, "you wouldn't. You're not an actress."

"No," said Noël, *"nor* a sentimentalist," and looked back at the screen.

At the end of the screening, and after drinks had been offered and congratulations extended, Miss Worth returned to the theme. "You called me a sentimentalist," she told Noël.

He nodded. "The play is one prolonged boxing match, and I don't feel tears are appropriate to it, somehow."

We stood together in a corner. "I am very proud of you," he said. "Don't worry about the interpolations, dear boy. I can't tell your dialogue from Dad's own. I never realized before that in this story I have said everything I *ever* learned about the theatre and everything I feel about it."

"Really? *Every*thing?"

"Give or take a few specific grudges." He winked, and in a moment was gone, escaping the crush of admirers and those who had wanted to say hello. One of the television executives had a private bit of information she had learned from a member of what she called "The Retinue." There was a new volume of Coward short stories, she had been told, soon to appear. "And," she whispered, "they're all about *death!*"

13

The various faces of death, of course, had shown themselves in much of Coward's later writing, in his short fictions written during the 1960's, in an unsuccessful play, *Waiting in the Wings,* set in a retirement home for elderly actresses, but nowhere so insistently as in his last major work, *A Song at Twilight.*

Death hangs over this final play like an avenging angel with time to spare. An after-dinner game for three players, the central figure is an elderly, world-famous author, Sir Hugo Latymer, who has no immediate plan for loosening his grip on life but is seen to be failing rapidly. As played by Coward himself, the character bore an astonishing resemblance to Maugham, with an occasional halting stammer and little nervous tics of the mouth; the burden of the story involving him is a threnody of emotional blackmail that is a marvel of elegant design and subtlety. An episode in his past must be acknowledged and dealt with. The possibility that Latymer may die before our very eyes without the conflict being brought to a resolution gives *A Song at Twilight* a sense of the greatest urgency that lifts it high above the level of a drawing-room drama, which in every other respect it resembles. All the commonplaces of polite drama enacted in elevated circumstances are present, but Coward's use of them, flamboyantly and always with a baleful humor, makes them seem like brand new merchandise of a very high order. Nowhere in the earlier plays is he more in command of his materials and nowhere has he been more deft in character delineation than in his last major work.

Yet it was presented as if it were not strong enough to stand on its own. It had to have two companion pieces to be played on the same bill on alternate nights with the major work, one of them no more than a slight entertainment and the second again about death. All three plays had a common setting: a hotel suite with a view of Lake Geneva. Undoubtedly the idea of a *tour de force* of such proportions, with Coward, Lilli Palmer and Irene Worth playing three different roles on two successive nights, was enormously attractive as a commercial proposition and the kind of *grand geste* that had not been seen in the contemporary theatre for decades. But its effect was to draw attention to the forest and its foliage, and the splendid, stately elm that is *A Song at Twilight* suffered in the camouflage.

It was following an evening performance of *A Song at Twilight* in May, 1966, that Noël and I sat in his dressing room at the Queen's Theatre, London, and managed to tell our news to each other as the steady inflow and outflow of reverential backstage visitors persisted in pairs: an eminent lady historian and her husband, two film stars, a distinguished journalist with a speech impediment and his sister, a French acting couple, an aging international dandy with his Alabama-born wife, both smelling strongly of whiskey and scent. Noël sat in great majesty, a patterned dressing gown over the shirt and trousers of the dinner clothes he had worn throughout the play, as if he expected his hand to be kissed by one and all. Something of the demeanor of Sir Hugo Latymer was still evident in his dressing-room self-presentation: a certain uncustomary hauteur mingled with a profound weariness. The weariness was not a part of the performance: he was insufficiently recovered from a severe and debilitating illness, and the role he had just played was a long and exhausting one. He was hoarse, and kept rolling a black-currant lozenge about on his tongue to refresh him while he smoked a cork-tipped cigarette and sipped a whiskey-and-soda.

His dresser, an amiable man with the sound of East London in his speech, poured out drinks in small measures as the callers made their congratulatory speeches and invited him to spend a quiet Sunday with them in the country; he accepted the praise courteously and declined all offers of bed and breakfast. Each semiprivate audience lasted no more than a few minutes, and even the French couple were conscious that others were waiting outside in the corridor and so refused the drink that was offered, saying that they had to hurry to supper.

At the end of the queue was the silver-haired dandy and his drawling magpie wife in black and white polka dots. The lady was still in tears, although the performance had ended at least twenty minutes earlier; with cheeks that seemed to be streaked with glycerine she repeated encomia: "Not since Laurette Taylor, Noël! I sweah! Not since Laurette Taylor in *The Glass Menagerie* herself has there been anything *like* it! Nothin' like it befoah or since, and only Laurette Taylor to compare it to. How *do* you *do* it?"

Noël put out his cigarette and rubbed a forefinger through his stage hairpiece. Beads of perspiration stood out on his brow. He searched himself in the mirror, perhaps for the answer to her question. "It is very tiring," he said. "It is not just a matter of saying the lines."

"Oh, but the *lines,*" she exclaimed. "What lines to say!" Her husband extended an eager hand to the dresser and accepted a neat whiskey in a plastic glass.

"And isn't Irene good?" he asked, his fingers beginning to work at the spirit gum caked on his brow where his false hair was anchored.

"And *Lilli,*" agreed the husband. "Lilli is *superb!*"

"Best thing she's evah done, that's all," the wife said.

"You must tell her," said Noël. "She'll be so pleased "

"I'll tell her tomorrow night, aftah we see the othah two plays. We can't wait for tomorrow night, Noël. I'm so excited! What parts do you play tomorrow night?"

"In one I play an American millionaire," he said, "and I worry a little about my accent."

"Oh, let's *hear* it. Give us a sample of it."

"Not now, dear," said the husband, "Noël must be terribly tired."

He offered a steely stare at his unsatisfactory reflection in the dressing-table mirror. "Would you like to come down to the country to us the first Sunday in July? I think Dickie Mountbatten is coming and there won't be anyone else. Just ourselves. We can have the car wait for you on the Saturday night before and drive you down."

Noël wheeled about in his chair and looked up at the man.

"*How* I should love to," he said, "but, alas, I speak literally to nobody from the time the curtain falls on Saturday night until it rises again the Monday evening following. Except to say 'Pass the mustard' or something equally imperative to a handmaiden. I think I might *just* manage to say, 'I smell smoke,' in the event someone had lit a fire under me; otherwise"—he moved his lips around the two syllables with a simulated asthmatic wheeze—*"nothing."*

Enriched Gigolo and Vintage Southern Belle departed. The dresser refreshed my drink and closed the door with a sigh, to which Noël answered, "Yes." The hairpiece came off and so did the dressing gown and stage trousers. All his movements were very slow and seemed to require deliberation beforehand.

"Do you happen to know where Tennessee Williams is at the moment?"

I thought he meant that he knew, that it was at an unlikely place, that he would tell me in a moment and expect me to laugh, or say that we were about to join Tennessee at the Caprice for supper. I said, "Where?"

"I don't know. I thought you might. I must telephone him. Tomorrow, perhaps. The Celebrity Service will know. In the past week I have been told three times that I can only be compared with Laurette Taylor in *The Glass Menagerie,* and I think the world at large must have an opportunity of judging for themselves if it is true. Therefore, after a suitable rest, I should like to undertake a season of *The Glass Menagerie* in New York and follow it with one in London. But I must have Tennessee's permission first. He might not see me as Amanda at all."

He extended his left arm and the dresser fixed a watch to Noël's wrist. A heavy application of cold cream erased, little by little, the stern aspect of Sir Hugo Latymer, and the familiar, friendly mandarin I knew as Noël Coward caught my eye in the looking glass. He also caught what may have seemed to him a look of dismay, for it had been sixteen years since I had seen him *en deshabille,* sixteen years since the swimming party in Connecticut.

Then, at fifty, he had been lithe and slender and as tan as a calfskin-bound book; limber and erect and as quick of movement as one-half of a professional dance team. Now, as he rose uncertainly from his chair to exchange the silk robe for a cotton one, the frame beneath the skin and sagging flesh was like something that had been taken apart and clumsily reassembled. The skin was yellowing and was marked here and there with light blue patches like bruises that are slow to heal.

He went to the washbasin to scrub himself with strong soap and cold water as the dresser dealt with the street clothes he would change into. When the toweling was done with and the alcohol rubbed into the muscles of his neck and shoulders had dried, he resumed his chair at the mirror and lit another cigarette.

"Since I last saw you," he said, "I nearly died."

I nodded gravely. I had from time to time sought news of his health from informed sources and had telephoned him at Les Avants-sur-Montreux on his previous birthday without being able to speak to him personally. He had been resting. The greetings were acknowledged by a letter from Cole Lesley, who wrote that the Master was "steadily improving," and behind that veiled admission of serious illness I detected at once a history that might never come to light.

"It seemed something like amebic dysentery," he went on, "caught in the Seychelle Islands, which drained practically every drop of my natural body fluids, and is why I look today like a particularly unappetizing prune. But one of the greatest diagnosticians in the world, in Rome, wrongly claimed that I had chronic colitis and put me on a diet of mashed potatoes and rice, exactly the wrong diet, you see, and that nearly finished me. But in Geneva the doctors rightly discovered that I have a spastic colon, and they ministered to me very well, so that I am able to do *this."* He waved his hand vaguely in the direction of the hairpiece on its stand, and gave a thin smile.

The term "spastic colon" is often a euphemism for cancer of any kind relating to the digestive system, and my own smile, intended to express great relief, evidently betrayed my thoughts.

"No, it's not cancer," he said, turning to the glass and employing a hairbrush, "but I am very weak. However, I shall be around for a while longer. Now, as they say in bad plays, let's talk of you."

The doyen of sixteen years earlier, the wise counselor of the young and uninitiated, saw himself in the dressing-room glass and recognized an old and familiar character he had once enjoyed playing. He buffed his nails with a chamois cloth pressed into a silver holder as he resumed an earlier attitude towards me, a pose of lofty admiration mingled with a faint disapproval. I had come over from Paris for two days to see him, and to see his plays; my clothes were newly French and my hair very long and barbered according to the prevailing fashion of the 8th and 16th arrondissements, a way of looking that was slow to cross the Channel unless imported by the very young. I had just turned forty-three, but, for the Master, nobody was ever too old to learn. For him, I was still in my twenties, the same young man with a crewcut and seersucker suit who had always to sit in the shade for fear of sun-poisoning, a neophyte with a loud laugh and a look of wanting to be thousands of miles away. I wanted to rip the Cardin jacket from my shoulders and snatch up a manicuring scissors from his dressing table to shear my hair down to its long-ago length. I was an impostor there, and time and luck had made me one; I ought properly to give him my telephone number, I thought, as being that of the Y.M.C.A. in the Tottenham Court Road and not the one he knew at the Ritz.

"Have they settled on a title for the movie you're doing in Paris?"

He knew what I was doing. It hadn't been mentioned. He always knew.

"There is still the awful French title, of course," I said, "but somebody will come up with a good one in English, because it's being done in English now. It turned out one of the stars speaks terrible French."

I did not mention the man's name. I didn't need to.

"Yes," he said, "it's curious, isn't it? After all that time that he lived in Paris, or *says* he lived there. On the other hand, does Romy Schneider speak English?"

I shrugged. The film I was working on—released as *Triple Cross*—was a costly World War II epic about an English safe-cracker who worked as a double agent for the Nazi High Command and the British Intelligence Service; there was very little fiction in the story that I had been called in to adapt from a talky French screenplay: the real-life hero of the piece had been given a full pardon by the Crown and was then living an uncamouflaged life in peacetime London. I was to meet him for the first time the following morning, and I said that I was looking forward eagerly to lunching with an arch-criminal.

"Are you going to his house or to a restaurant?" Noël wanted to know.

"To his house. I think it is in Montagu Square."

"Some of the most beautiful rooms in London. *Very* baroque taste, but quite uniquely beautiful. Lots of Russian enamel picture frames and clocks, and fire-screens of Queen Anne embroidery. Two very large dogs and a mistress. You'll enjoy him."

"You *know* him?" My astonishment was real.

"I've been to his house, yes. It is not the *least* unrespectable

202

to go there. He knows everybody. I thought at first that of course he'd had some decorator do it all up for him, but no, every smidgin of it is in his own taste. I conclude that good taste must be a natural concomitant of great larceny. A fine thief must know what is fine before he steals it. I suppose they're paying you a great deal for rescuing them from that script they had?"

I said I thought the remuneration was more than satisfactory.

"I'm delighted to hear it." He extended his empty glass to the dresser and indicated that my own needed refilling. "Then perhaps you'll be able to afford to take a year off and set to work on a novel."

He said it as a conjecture, but the slightly interrogatory reading of the words contained an implicit reproach, reviving an ancient and favorite *rengaine* between us that I was a born novelist and should make it my business to do nothing else but write fiction of some length and purpose. The only novel I'd written had been published five years before and had convinced him of this, but he had initiated the old refrain as early as 1955, and had repeatedly resung it at regular intervals after my first travel articles had begun to appear in various magazines.

We sipped our drinks for a little while without speaking. He seemed not to want to hurry off to bed at the Savoy, and Coley and Graham were somewhere having supper with friends; a pleasant stillness had settled upon the welcome and rare occasion of being alone with Noël. The dresser busied himself with coat hangers and clothes brushes in efficient silence.

"I thought," I said, "I might go to Deauville in the month of August, when the rest of them are doing the interior scenes in the studio down in Nice."

"You can't begin a novel in Deauville in the month of August," he said. "They wouldn't permit it."

"I don't know a soul there," I protested.

"Because there aren't any. But the polo crowd and all those divorcées and *jeunes hommes ambigus* will take you up in twenty minutes and you'll be in the Casino every night until dawn."

"And, anyway, I don't have a novel in my head."

He sighed and turned back again to the glass and resumed the activity with the fingernail buffer for want of something to do with his hands.

"I want to warn you about too much urbanity. It is not the first time I have said this. I said this to you many years ago at Jack Wilson's house in Fairfield. I've said it to you on other occasions. And Charley Laughton told me *he* had said the same thing to you."

There it was again, the "urbanity" lecture.

At first, that day at Sardi's restaurant when we had been unmindful of the time and were too late for the start of a Joan Crawford movie, the "urbanity" lecture may have had some bearing on my deportment: I had defended myself then as one who worked and thought best at night, who found companions in the great world stimulating and instructive, and that it ought to be everybody's private business how and where and when he got his work done. Later, after the years in London and Paris and the obscure retreats I found on the Continent, it had very little application to me, yet the lecture was resumed with every emphasis intact nearly every time we met. It struck me one day that perhaps Noël was not addressing *me* at all, that the speech was made essentially for his own benefit, in the way that someone will tie a string around his finger as an *aide-mémoire*. I had once known a very old spinster of great riches and nearly legendary refinement who had no other counsel for the young ladies of Philadelphia, where she lived, than that they must in no circumstances be seen with bare hands in any public place, in restaurants or at concerts or sporting events. She spoke, they said, of little else. When people recall her fondly, it is always as the lady who had so many pairs of gloves that they filled an entire armoire, yet she was never to be seen wearing them when she went out.

It was little more than speculation on my part, but I now wonder if it might not have been compulsory for Noël to spell out the dangers of "urbanity" and extravagance as a cautionary reminder that he had long ago learned the unwisdom of waste and excess, and was in need of hearing it all confirmed again even if he had to say it himself. If so, it could be said that he followed his own advice scrupulously. Wherever I understood its reference to me I tried to follow it as best I could.

"Cities are there to be enjoyed when one needs them," he said, "as stimulating people are. I adore Rebecca West because whenever I see her she makes me *think*. She invigorates me. But a diet of her several times a week would be fattening. I should feel sluggish and not want to work. Have you not thought of going away to some quiet village in France and settling into it for a few months?"

I had and said so. I identified the place as Lyons-la-Forêt, in the middle of a beech forest a half hour from Rouen, where Ravel had gone to write *Daphnis and Chloe*.

"Don't know it. What was it like in Greece?"

"There was no urbanity there at all," I said defensively. I had stayed seven months the year before in a small house near the sea front of Paralia, a suburb of Kalamata, in the southern Peloponnesus, where I had worked on the television plays. The environment had been thoroughly agreeable and conducive to hard work, bucolic and salutary and, finally, monotonous. I told him about it, and added, "It was every bit as provincial as New York."

I told him about boarding my getaway plane, an Alitalia jet, at Athens and experiencing an almost mystic joy when a bottle of Beaujolais was served with the lunch tray, a noontime ecstasy compounded of the pleasant prospect of a return to Continental Europe and the shock to the palate of drinking a wine that had actually been grown and not hastily fermented in a resinated barrel.

"I experienced a similar strong emotion when I drank a cup of English tea for the first time after much too long in China," he said, and held out his empty glass for refreshing. "Well, certainly the food in Greece is an endurance contest that nobody wins, but I believe that in Turkey it's even worse. Now, where are you putting up in Paris?"

I ought to have said that I was staying with friends, in the rue de l'Université, or in a small and charming hotel near the Invalides, but the truth was that I was sumptuously housed in an *hôtel de luxe* and fully enjoying the attentions of the floor service for breakfast, lunch and, sometimes, dinner while pages issued forth from the typewriter and were taken away, two or three at a time, by a messenger to be photocopied. The floor of my bedroom was carpeted in Savonnerie and overcarpeted in numbered sheets of paper, assorted in piles of shell pink, French blue and a sickly violet, the colors of the pages being an index to a calendar of cinema production the producer's secretary had originated in the nearly vain hope that she might retain her sanity. The Louis Quinze reproductions, commodes, chairs and credenzas were piled high with reference works in three languages; the accommodation overlooked a courtyard overwrought with plane and chestnut trees and had clearly been realized with someone of a quiet and retiring disposition in mind, but now it was a workroom and late-night conference rendezvous, finger-marked and loud with typewriting, smelling of cheap French tobacco and expensive beer, Guerlain soap and a bunch of white lilac that had withered of thirst and no chambermaid had thought to remove. Could I tell him this? Could I say that I was staying in one of the costliest hotels in the world because everyone else connected with the film was there as well? Would it carry conviction to say that the producer's suite was one floor below me and that I could scurry down the servants' stairs in pajamas and robe, if I had a question that needed an immediate answer there, without being seen? Could I say that the producer's secretary had a tiny oubliette there with a bed and a washbasin and paid for sleeping in what had once been a sewing room out of her own pocket because it saved her so much time and vexation? I felt that his view of me and of the uncertainty of my livelihood, insofar as he was familiar with the details of my subsistence, did not admit of my living high off the hog, and any hesitation in giving my address might well have made the reply seem a dishonest one. To equivocate with Noël was unthinkable. I named the hotel.

"Quite right," he said. "With the kind of pressure you must be working under it's the only place, really. Are you in the back or the front?"

The dresser poured out another drink for me at a signal from the Master. I explained to him the nature of the quite out-of-the-ordinary task I had been given. A long-projected film to be made in the French language with a large cast of international stars had, until a short time before, lacked half of its financing. Three million dollars had surprisingly fallen into the producers' laps from a major Hollywood film company, with the provision that the film be made in English. No delay in the production schedule was possible: three of the actors had pressing commitments to be filled elsewhere at the end of ten weeks, and Romy Schneider, the leading actress, was noticeably five months' pregnant. Having earned a not entirely justified reputation for working rapidly and coherently under stress, I was assigned to the job of writing the English-language screenplay in a sequence dictated by a production schedule made even more confused by the need to film all of Miss Schneider's scenes first without reference to the economic practicality of so doing. This meant that the scenario had to be written back-to-front, so to speak, in that many of the actress's scenes came at the very end of the story and the rest of them only at the very beginning. Nor was it simply a matter of putting a French text into English. Miss Schneider, an intelligent woman with a good command of several languages, saw at once that the complex and ambiguous character she was to play had been treated only superficially by the French author; a Norwegian noblewoman educated at Vassar at the expense of the Nazis ought to speak English dialogue that reflected something of her contradictory nature and the unusual history that had produced it. As I rewrote it in English, her character developed in such a way that her role took on an importance in the story it had not previously had and put Christopher Plummer, her romantic vis-à-vis, in the cinematic shade. The latter, an actor with an intelligence equal to Miss Schneider's own, thereupon insisted that a similar improvement be made in his own role, and, following a pattern of monkey-see-monkey-do behavior as familiar to film studios as to the nursery, his male co-star followed suit. The director was Terence Young, a highly proficient Englishman with the educated man's love of language, who encouraged them and me in this full-scale revision of the screenplay, and I found myself writing and rewriting scenes to accommodate changes made in the scenes that would not be filmed for weeks to come in a disorder to which the words "total confusion" are the only ones applicable.

Noël relished this history and smacked his lips pleasurably at my evident consternation. The dresser laughed aloud and shook his head in wonderment at the vagaries of the entertainment world beyond Shaftsbury Avenue; there, under his regimentation, not even a matchbox was out of place.

The theatre had acquired the modifier "legitimate" because it was a place of order and dignity in contrast with the slapdash worlds of the circus and the music hall, and Noël himself, possibly, shared this view. The idea of back-to-front composition, of scenes written to be played in a garden suddenly rewritten to be played in a baroque interior because the weather was threatening; the whole notion of a race with the stork, amused him mightily. I had never seen him quite so relaxed or eager to hear more, and though it was nearly midnight and the dresser apparently wished to be somewhere else, Noël encouraged me not to stop. I murmured something about "the trees" and, deciding that the history of a single tree branch was unworthy of his attention, went on to say something else.

"What trees, dear boy? I want to hear about the trees. Don't, whatever you do, leave out the trees!"

About a third of the film I was working on was to be shot at a fine old château near Meulan-la-Jolie, no more than an hour's drive to the southwest of Paris. Set in a park that had been laid out by LeNotre, the château was a great white elephant to its owners, titled members of an ancient family who lived there in circumstances that very few people in modern times could afford. The gardens alone required a team of nine landscapers and their numerous assistants in biweekly attendance to preserve LeNotre's symmetry, and the advent of a film unit, with its trucks and generators and dressing-rooms-on-wheels, created hazards that were totally unforeseen by the unwordly aristocrats in residence, delighted with the flow of American dollars into their account. They had asked for, and received in advance, a stupendous sum for opening their gates to the cinema, but their sole foresight had been in demanding a policy of insurance that would indemnify them dou-bly for even the slightest alteration to the stately and formal look of their domain.

The access to the château and its floral environs was a mile-long avenue, double-edged with espaliered oak trees that had sur-vived two centuries of artistic tree surgery and, in summer and early autumn, had their leaves trimmed back daily in such a way that the illusion of two lines extending to a vanishing point, when seen from the entrance gate, was harmoniously preserved. On the very first morning of actual film work on the château grounds a huge truck bearing camera equipment and electrical apparatus lurched sideways and knocked off the lowest branch of the last and the noblest tree. Madame la Marquise had come running out in bedroom attire and a state of panic to see the fallen limb; she wept as dramatically as if the amputation had been performed on her own distinguished person. The Lloyds of London people were there within the hour and saw in minutes that any financial assessment of the loss of the tree branch, when seen as the keynote or the cornerstone of a grand design incorporating thousands of identical branches and more than a million leaves, was a matter only a Solomon could settle. Bourbon hysteria flooded the scene; in Madame's opinion there could now be no question of film being exposed on her premises, of a clapper-boy speaking searchingly into a lens the number of a scene and a take, of ersatz Nazis with swastika armbands goose-stepping on her lawns, no question un-less an answer could be supplied that would please the Credit Lyonnais and Monsieur le Marquis himself. Unsurprisingly, it took a practical Frenchwoman, assigned to remedy Romy Schneider's makeup when the occasion warranted, to come up with a solution: the fallen branch should be copied in papier-mâché, treated with a weatherproofing substance and attached to the tree trunk with metal braces. Several facsimiles should be made, not only one, to reproduce the look of the bicentenarian branch at every season of the year, and substituted at the appropriate time. The cosmetician was invited into the innermost fastnesses of the chateau for refreshment and gracious expressions of thanks.

Noël found this tale hilarious and shook with merriment over it; I had never seen him so amused. He was barely able to articulate his only comment: "An eye for an eye and a limb for a limb!"

I had other anecdotes to tell about the moviemaking scene in Paris, and he heard them all with an amiable acknowledgment of the capricious nature of the business, though he shook his head in wonderment at certain excesses of temperament in the behavior of actors he had known and worked with and even genuinely admired. A man who first came to prominence in a film Noël wrote had experienced a number of personal tragedies in rapid succession and found solace only in whiskey; he was playing an important, if brief, role in the film I was writing. At the mention of the man's name, Noël covered his eyes with his hand. Mistaking the gesture for an expression of weariness, I rose to go. But he uncovered his eyes and nodded in such a way that I sat down again.

"Avoid him!" he exclaimed. "He will drain every bit of energy that is left in you, and take you out on the town, to all the late-night spots, and charm you with his unreliable memories of the war and what fun it all was, and at the evening's end you will find that you have paid dearly for it, not only from your pocketbook but in the wasted energy of listening to one of the most engaging talkers in the world. Your mind will wander back to what he was saying when it should only be on your business, which is to get on with the goddamned movie!"

Weeks later, heedless of his instructions, I was unavoidably thrust into exactly the kind of nocturnal revelry he foresaw, and during the two days thereafter was uncharacteristically disabled at my work.

"Now let's talk about me," he said airily. "What do you think of Dad's Renaissance?"

Hay Fever was still the outstanding magnet of the National Theatre's repertory, *Present Laughter* had been the previous tenant at the Queen's Theatre, a new volume of short stories had just been announced for publication, revivals of *Fallen Angels* and *Private Lives* were in the works, *The Vortex* had been exhumed in the provinces, and the television series of his short stories was then in production. The late Sean Kenny, one of the most gifted and imaginative scenic designers ever to astonish the eyes of London theatregoers, an elfin Irishman with a wicked tongue, had dignified the whole movement with the published words: "The London theatre is finished. There's a Noël Coward Renaissance, for God's sake!"

"Is 'Renaissance' your word for the play I saw tonight?" I asked.

"Or Mr. Sean Kenny's. Have you something to say about it?"

I said that I thought it a major achievement and one whose excellence would not be appreciated even by those who welcomed it most. The shimmering stylishness of the ensemble acting and the graceful manner of the play's execution served in some ways to conceal the remarkable dramaturgy and the measured cadences of the scenes. In *A Song at Twilight*, an entire dinner is eaten center-stage: firkins of caviar, stout filets mignons and salad, plates of chocolate mousse. There is no sense of hurry to the meal; it is, in fact eaten in a leisurely manner, as if neither of the diners had much appetite for it. The food is consumed during a cat-and-mouse scene of exceptional cleverness and wit; the long-ago mistress is reluctant to name her weapons or declare open warfare until coffee and brandy have been served. Throughout the dinner there is a strong sense of imminent unpleasantness that is only heightened by the almost casual activity of eating, and the tension mounts with each mouthful. Yet the dinner, eaten at a pace that would seem like the normal one to any member of the audience, occupies no more than twelve minutes of the actors' time. The consummate skill with which Noël and Lilli Palmer played this intricate, busy scene and timed their movements was artifice transformed into art of the very highest order. It was also taken to be a stunt, like something from a magician's paraphernalia, and the audience buzzed with pleasure during the interval at what they had just seen, as if the art they had been observing was prestidigitation and not that of playwriting. I pointed this out to him as an illustration of what I meant.

"They *do* enjoy that," he said, looking like a self-satisfied pussycat, "because the scene is very deceptive. And, by the way, unbe*lie*vably difficult to do. If the laugh doesn't come on one of my lines and Lilli has got her mouth full of salad, she can't come in with her line until she's swallowed it, and the imperceptible pause spoils the rhythm of the scene. I tried a little trick with my serviette tonight, did you notice? I may embellish that in the future. It seems to cover an awkward bit of chewing."

"Do you really *eat* that dinner? It doesn't look at all like stage food." "It is. Apples and Grape Nuts, mostly. You know English actors. We can make a banquet out of a *biscuit.*"

It was always unwise to make references to the critical fraternity in general or one of its brethren in particular in Noël's presence; his dislike of them was boundless and his respect for them nonexistent. He found both their praise and their blame to be harmful. Newcomers were overpraised only to the detriment of their subsequent writing or acting performances, and established theatricians were punished for not being the shoemakers who stuck to their lasts. He was infuriated by the omnipotence of the newspaper critics in New York, believing that their influence was in inverse proportion to their knowledge, and he once described Brooks Atkinson and Walter Kerr as the "unhidden persuaders." Yet the press for the three plays then in season at the Queen's had been sober and appreciative; the high-minded Sunday *Observer*, always scornful of light offerings with a whiff of Belgravia in them and mocking of serious ones set in surroundings *de luxe*, compared the Master to Sartre, and the three figures of *A Song at Twilight* with those in *No Exit*. Another intellectual nay-sayer in a different weekend paper called Noël "the greatest theatrical entertainer of our century," and a third executed journalistic handsprings in an eloquent paean that was an effort to describe that elusive element in his work most people mistakenly call "style." Reading the reviews in Paris the previous Sunday, I had been exhilarated that the pendulum had swung, inevitably, back; that what "Dad" called his "Renaissance" was really on, and in full swing. Pendulums are never still until the clock has stopped. I mentioned having read the reviews and delivered myself of my little aphorism about the pendulum.

"Yes," he said, examining the toes of his shoes for offending dust, "and even a stopped clock is right twice in twenty-four hours."

There was a discursion then dealing with the merits of Kenneth Tynan as a critic ("more perceptive than anyone in my memory, but too fond of too-long words") and a brisk dismissal of Beverley Nichols's book on Maugham ("I had no idea there was so much gold to be found down in Somerset"), one of his double-edged cracks that had the sound of having been tried out on others first.

The dresser switched off some of the lights, and Noel rose to be helped into a plum-colored blazer, be brushed off with a whisk and have his pockets checked. Keys, cigarettes and lighter were accounted for and some pound notes crumpled into a wad and stuffed into his trousers pocket. A mackintosh was draped over the back of a chair, and the dresser said good night as Noël sat down again and refreshed his drink; his thoughts had returned to my duties in Paris.

"Of course, you're exercising a good many new muscles this way, and there's never any harm in that." He waited a moment, and ran his forefinger over the edge of a Kleenex box. "But, frankly, I don't like the look of you. I don't mean the long hair, which is a mere caprice you'll soon tire of. You have a look of worry, and disappointment, and also of fatigue, which is perfectly understandable. Is something else the matter?"

Romy Schneider had put her finger on it that very day at lunch. My ambitions for rescuing the film script from the swamp of mediocrity that was its current, shapeless condition far exceeded my abilities to persuade anyone connected with the enterprise that a really fine movie was waiting to be made. Romy had given a little Austrian sigh of weariness over her artichoke and told me that I was an idealist. I had protested. I said that the movie was based on a real-life adventure lived by fascinating and eccentric people of ambiguous national loyalties and that their natures had suffered a kind of attrition in their transfer to paper. We were likely to finish with a comic strip peopled by pen-and-ink sketches, and that the time to forestall such a thing happening was then and there, with only a few days of actual filming already completed. She had patted my hand in an encouraging way and wished me luck.

"Fight," said Noël, when I repeated this to him. "Always fight for it, if you believe in it. Even hackwork wants a certain conviction, and also passion."

The words stung. Rewriting another man's work to a schedule was not what I had set out to do in life. It was the first time I had done it.

But the rewards were handsome and out of all proportion to the achievement. The climate of activity was new to me and stimulated my imagination. A limousine with chauffeur at my disposal was seductive; I longed for more free time to enjoy it. The great cuisine of Parisian restaurants was now my daily fare. There would be other films coming along later in the year that needed my surgery and suturing and would perpetuate the comforting circumstances I now enjoyed. That this was the life, and the occupation, of a "hack," albeit a very expensive one, shamed me and made me blush to hear him say it. The image of him, the "Master-of-all-trades," as he had been called, the legend in his lifetime, indulging me in a monologue of trivial complaints while he sat there, depleted of energy and vocally exhausted, insufficiently recovered from an illness that might have written a full stop to his career as an actor and had interrupted his writing and composing, was a blistering reproach to any self-esteem that might survive the evening.

"Passion?" I asked, for want of something better to say, and helped myself to some more whiskey.

"Oh, yes, *passion*. Passion will keep the pot on the boil!"

"If there's no other fuel? Is that what you mean?"

"Dear boy, do you think I *wanted* to go and sing for the customers at Wilbur Clark's Desert Inn? It was the money. I needed the money. It came in very handy. Very handy, indeed. I reckoned that I had numerous shortcomings to expose to that Las Vegas crowd and that the only thing to do was to make the best of it, which I am happy to say I did. When I arrived there I believe there were exactly nine people in the state of Nevada who knew my name, and five of *them* thought I was dead. Two others thought I was Rex Harrison. Weeks later I had become a household word, because I had *amused* them. It was most gratifying."

"Then you were *passionate* at Las Vegas?"

"About the money, chiefly. In the desert, I find, money is the only thing that excites the senses. Think of all those ancient prospectors. Help Dad up from this chair. We must go now." I helped him into his mackintosh and he took my arm for support; the weight of him was noticeably greater than it had been that day in Capri eighteen months earlier when he had taken my arm on the waterfront and I had first been conscious of the weakness in his legs. In the person of Sir Hugo Latymer, on the stage that night, his walk had been that of an old, enfeebled man. I now realized that the gifts of a fine actor had played no part in that uncertain gait and that the uncustomary hesitancy of his movements was not imaginative characterization but a very real physical debility.

The steps leading from the dressing room to the stage door presented no problem; he used the rail to his one side for stability. But helping him into the waiting taxi offered difficulties of balance that the stage doorman was better equipped to deal with than I, and the doorman when we reached the Savoy was quick to meet his familiar responsibility in getting Noël out of the cab at the hotel entrance.

We stood there for a moment at the revolving doors under the porte-cochère in the fine spring night, prolonging a handshake that expressed so many unspoken things. He seemed to want to sum up, to encapsulate what he had been saying in the dressing room, and I waited. His summation was an old maxim of the theatre, born of anguish and disappointment and worry.

"Remember," he said, "that nobody *asked* you to be in show business."

I walked back to the Ritz the longer way, via the Strand and Pall Mall and past the sleeping St. James's, repeating the old saw, which an eminent American playwright had seen fit to have printed for him in bold type and affixed to the wall where he could look at it while he worked. It offered no solace, neither did it admonish. It looked the condition of professionalism squarely in the face and said, "Get on with it." If that was Noël's message to me, his counsel would be well taken.

14

The following evening was a different kind of occasion altogether. A driving rainfall had dampened every theatregoer in Shaftesbury Avenue, and the audience for the other two plays in *Suite in Three Keys* was slow to come to attention and fidgeted uncomfortably with rainwear and umbrellas, handbags and programs throughout the first twenty minutes. Noël's greeting on his first entrance was a sustained round of applause which seemed to signal their readiness to concentrate, but it was uphill work for him, and for the two actresses, to engage them fully in the geometry of the triangle he had constructed with imminent death rather than sexual infidelity as its hypotenuse.

Shadows of the Evening is a stiff-upper-lip play and, like its companion piece, moves forward in the same setting where, the night before, Sir Hugo Latymer, his German-born wife and a former mistress had waged a civilized war in which honesty was the only possible victor. The second evening began instead with honesty, the necessity of facing squarely the reality that George Hilgay, a prominent English publisher, would die in a month or two and, following fits of weeping that seized both his first and second wives, proceeded to a slightly tipsy and even light-hearted acceptance of the outcome as the trio prepared themselves for an evening of gambling at Evian. It was impossible for me, in the light of our long friendship and more particularly in the cruel light of the dressing-room interlude the night before, to view the play as anything but its author's struggle to come to terms with growing old in a gallant and even flippant way. The publisher, as Noël played him, dapper and very much of-the-moment, given to clipped pronunciamentos and longish speeches involving the hereafter plus the distinct possibility of its nonexistence, was a figure I took to be the matured heroes of the light comedies I had seen when I was a schoolboy all rolled into one: Elyot had heard the riot act read aloud and a waspish Amanda had come to complain that he saw so little of the children; Joanna, of a later vintage, had acquired an understanding that present laughter did not endure and only tears ever displaced it; Simon Gayforth had stepped into darker shadows of the evening than he ever dreamed of in the company of the elusive, suicide-bent Victoria. The continuousness of Coward's heroes as their melodies were played out in a minor key became the subject and even the argument of the evening: it was in this way, and this way only, that the comedy of forty years and more could be concluded. The performance, beautifully executed by the trio, adjusting every nuance to the desultory mood of the audience, enhanced the extra-theatrical meaning that could be found in it:

Lilli Palmer, awash in tears from time to time, achieved a melancholy confusion of emotions that seemed to me to have more to do with Noël as a man and the evident foreshortening of the days we would be able to spend with him than it did with his impersonation of the stage husband she faced; hers was a moving enactment of an anticipated grief which transmitted itself rapidly if unemphatically to a scattered handful of spectators. A woman near me was sobbing uncontrollably at the end.

"Hardly *like* a Noël Coward play at all," said a man in the stalls bar during the interval.

"We're all getting older, dear," said the lady with him.

When the curtain rose on the second half of the evening, the stage was filled with a simulated sunlight and there was no threat that the Grim Reaper was waiting in the wings. Irene Worth, herself American-born, was playing a hennaed matron from the Southwest done up in pin curlers, and Noël was her millionaire husband. His silvering crewcut hairpiece gave him the look of a Pentagon dignitary in mufti and his accent was a medley of Chicago, Texas and St. Louis; it seemed likely that the character had been educated in Brooklyn. *Come into the Garden, Maud* was instantly recognizable for what it was, an amusing romp with three lively caricatures, prefabricated objects of hostility guaranteed to elicit extravagant laughter from a British audience; funny, uneducated accents alone would do this.

The piece had inherited its subject matter from Sinclair Lewis's *Dodsworth,* its naïve-Yankee-in-corrupt-old-Europe point of view from its author's long-felt admiration for Henry James. The materials had been coarsened both in the writing and in the playing, however, in a way that astonished me; as a curtain-raiser to a serious work it would have been an insubstantial time-marker; as the wind-up of a trilogy of plays, one of which was a major work, it was a larkish revue sketch woefully needing to be augmented with songs. The acting was of an exaggerated kind for which the epithet "vaudeville" would not have been ill-chosen. There was a courting of laughter that was little more than pandering to the audience and a tendency for the two women to play their scenes directly front, a style of acting perfectly suitable to the plays of Neil Simon, where the dialogue hurries on from joke to joke, but totally out of place in a play by Noël Coward, as it would be in one by Bernard Shaw.

Moreover, the plot was preposterous. Lilli Palmer played a Roman noblewoman, emancipated from the strict Italian *borghese* environment she despised, who was visiting Geneva to await the birth of her first grandchild. The parents of the imminent offspring were deftly drawn in a few lines referring to them and made so interesting and real that programs were inspected in the vain hope that they would not remain offstage. Romance between the liberated *principessa* and the American moneybags erupted as surprisingly and inappropriately as to suggest that at least one or two preparatory scenes for this development had been omitted at that evening's performance. There was no accounting for it, I felt, and nothing anywhere in Coward's work, not even in the unproduced and immature *Home Chat,* to explain the carelessness of its structure, or the fact that its resolution—the flight of the man to an autumnal adventure with an improbable and probably penniless aristocrat in her elderly, tiny Fiat—had been uncomfortably telegraphed to even the dullest member of that evening's audience forty minutes before it came to pass. The experience was personally insufferable, and I did something I have only rarely ever done: I left my aisle seat and went to stand at the back of the stalls of the Queen's Theatre to see the rest of the play out; in the world of the theatre this is an act of discourtesy for which no imaginative excuse can be offered; if the actors themselves do not actually see the premature departure, the empty seat tells all.

From my position at the back, with my arms folded across a curtained railing, the stage activity lost its immediacy and I was able to watch Noël and his chosen ladies as figures in a bright shadow box performing a ceremonial enactment of the end of a marriage.

"Good night, sweetheart" had been established early in the play as the husband's traditional end-of-the-evening words before retiring to his bedroom for the night. Lest the ritualistic nature of this escape the audience, the words were repeated again midway through the action. Playwrights are uncommonly alert to the sound of repeated words: the first repetition invariably means that there will be a second, according to an ancient principle called "the rule of three," and I thought I could accurately foretell what the curtain line would be.

Sure enough, the lights were dimmed and stage moonlight illuminated the scene as Noël made his preparations to walk out on his wife and fly to the embrace of Lilli Palmer in the waiting Fiat. He went to the door of his wife's bedroom and paused there; the wait took on a dramatic importance; the breakneck pace of the comedy had come to a dead halt, as if a noisy clock had suddenly stopped. "Good night, sweetheart," he said, and turned to go. The curtain fell.

Throughout the curtain calls my eyes were dim with tears; the final speech had been so neatly prepared for that I was sure it was intended to have an extra-theatrical meaning, his *"ave atque vale"* to one and all. I knew as I stood there that I was applauding an entire career and not a single performance, and that I would never see him act again.

Before going backstage as I had promised, I had a double

whiskey in the saloon bar of a dingy, crowded place referred to by the actors who frequent it as "The French Pub." A middle-aged man with the sound of Glasgow in his speech stood beside me, clutching a pint of lager in one hand and a program for the Queen's Theatre in the other; seeing an identical program rolled up in my own hand was enough to establish a basis for conviviality.

"What'd you think of it, then?"

"I liked the first one," I said. "I'm not sure about the second one."

"He's smashing, though, in the second one, sendin' up the Yanks that way. I thought he *liked* Yanks. Bit nasty, some of that. Are you a Yank?"

I nodded.

"Didn't offend you, that anti-Americanism, or what you might call it?"

I said I thought in fact the play celebrated a kind of American innocence in the character Noël played, at the same time it attacked the vulgar snobbery of the newly rich in the person of the man's wife.

"I reckon I've seen him in everything," said the Scotsman, "since during the war. Smashing actor. Wonder he never did do Shakespeare. Voice too light perhaps."

I turned to face him. His remark implied a sophistication sharply at variance with the way he looked. An understanding of vocal limitations is generally only that of actors themselves, rarely that of a layman. I was about to ask if he was an actor while I ordered another whiskey and a lager from the man behind the bar.

"Death, death, death," said the presumed actor, "in last night's play, and more in the first one tonight. But the second one tonight takes the curse off the other two. Oh, it's nothing but tuppenny exaggeration, mind you, and won't stand up to real inspection. But that Italian lady, you notice, has come all the way from Rome in her little car, which is quite a distance, to make sure her kid's kid is born okay. Now that kid of hers is some kind of a 'hippie,' as they say in your country, and a 'flower person', and if I get the picture correctly, her daughter-in-law is nae much different. And at the end, the grandchild has been born in the hospital alive and well, and what does the new father go and do the first thing? Has his hair cut off. Probably going out to look for work tomorrow, and needin' to look respectable. So Mister Coward is sayin' somethin' to us all: some of us have reached the end of the road but a baby was born tonight. And that baby might just possibly, stretching it a bit, grow up to be another Noël Coward. Or at any rate an entertainer. Even a good one. Two plays about the end of life, and the last one about the beginning of it. Smashing good work, really. Now that I come to think of it.''

I had not thought of the plays except as three different exercises; the experience was too recent for me to see the overall design and to understand, as I came to do only very much later, the significance of the buffoonery in the last work. I said good night to the Scotsman and crossed the street to the stage alley.

The corridor leading to Noël's dressing room was lined on both sides with waiting visitors and loud with voices in which excited and congratulatory tones could already be heard. I lit a cigarette and stood at the end of the queue. The dresser came down the corridor with a tweed jacket on a coat hanger. He smiled at me and said he would tell the Master I was waiting, and a moment later Cole Lesley came out to shake my hand and say how sorry he was to have missed seeing me the night before.

"He's very, very tired tonight, Bill," he added. "Did you keep him up very late last night?"

"I suppose it was late, yes, Coley," I said. "But he didn't seem to want to go home."

"I know how you two are when you get to talking," he said kindly. "Best come round some other evening soon."

"I have to be back in Paris in the morning."

"Oh. Well, pop in then just to say hello."

"No, I'll try to come over again in a week or so. Tell Noël his American accent is fine."

"I will. You're looking very tired, Bill. Keeping late hours?"

I told him briefly about the strains of my duties in Paris, and he nodded with full understanding.

"Just remember what the Master always says: 'It's nice to be working.' "

We said good night then and I went back to the Ritz, with two of "Dad's" thoughts to comfort me, the one Coley had just repeated and the one from the night before. The thing to do was simply to get on with it.

15

There were two Holy Weeks in the year 1969, at least in London. The first was the annual one of the Lenten season, the second was sanctified and given its name by the man in whose honor it was observed.

It began on the eve of Noël's seventieth birthday with a midnight performance at the Phoenix Theatre, scene of so many of his early triumphs, succeeded by seven days of celebrations, banquets, tributes and nightly performances of his plays and songs on television. An editorial in *The Times* said that if there was a single man, woman or child in the United Kingdom who did not by the week's end know the name of Noël Coward his ignorance was beyond the reach of the mass media. One of the intellectual weeklies remarked upon the irreverence of the Bank of England when it failed to close its doors to business on the birthday itself. Department stores in Regent Street devoted window displays to Coward memorabilia, Gertrude Lawrence's white Molyneux dress from *Private Lives* was cheaply adapted and sold well, the piped-music service heard in restaurants and airlines terminals played "Zigeuner" and "I'll See You Again" together with some of the less well known songs as if no other composer of light music had ever existed.

It is often said of the English that they have a special knack for celebration and no equals when doing homage to their native sons; their love for great occasions and pageantry is only exceeded by their weakness for self-congratulation when one of their great men, homegrown on the tight little island, wins the Nobel prize, circles the earth in a sailboat, or achieves a ripe old age. Then the banners and the bunting are unfurled, the diamond necklaces come out of the vaults and the sound of cheering is heard through the land.

The gala at the Phoenix Theatre was months in preparation and weeks in rehearsing. A consolidation of theatrical charities, of which one, the Actors' Orphanage, had long enjoyed Noël's personal attention, benefited from the occasion. Invitations were sent out long beforehand and seats distributed democratically: the larger the contribution, the better they were located. Only members of the royal party, led by the Princess Margaret, had extraordinary accommodations at the front of the balcony; Noël himself, escorting Merle Oberon, sat in what on other occasions would have been the royal box, with Graham and Coley and two other great friends, Gladys Calthrop and Joyce Carey.

The festive nature of the night established itself in the street outside with police barricades, klieg lights and sidewalk entertainers in the traditional button-studded costumes of the London "busker." The BBC television news service had stayed up long past its bedtime to transmit on-the-spot interviews with the more celebrated celebrants as they stepped from their limousines; and at the end of the red carpet, in the lobby, a glass of champagne waited for everyone. The gilt paper covers of the programs bore the Coward autograph and were protected from finger marks by a folder of clear celluloid that identified them as something no one would wish to discard.

Midnight matinees, as the London theatrical community calls them, are notoriously late in starting; not so this one. Noël appeared in the box in his chocolate-brown tuxedo promptly at twelve and waved a greeting to the audience that silenced applause. The royal party's arrival seconds later brought them to their feet as the anthem was played, and the marathon entertainment had commenced.

Four and a half hours later, with only a fifteen-minute pause for refreshment in between, the Princess rose to lead a standing ovation that an elderly journalist wrote was the most prolonged since Victoria had waved from her wheelchair on the day of her diamond jubilee. The night had seen nothing but excellence. The words and music were familiar, and so were the performers. Representatives of generations unborn when Coward was thirty sang his forty-year-old songs as if they had just been minted and were having their first hearing. Old friends appeared in new guises: Joyce Grenfell, a monologist and broad comedienne whose aunt was Lady Astor, pulled out a gilt ball-chair, spread her peachbloom-pink organza skirt around her and sat with her hands folded, gazing wistfully up at the box to sing "Heigh-Ho, If Love Were All."

A light-skinned black woman who had made a handsome marriage and retired from the stage many years before returned from rich obscurity to sing "Twentieth Century Blues" in a voice that was the equal of any blues singer of the century, a concoction of cream and molasses, and created a stir of whispering and conjecture as to her identity; she had asked that her name not appear on the program. A female impersonator, Danny La Rue, then the object of an adoring cult, dressed himself up to look like a plump Marlene Dietrich and sang "I've Been to a Marvelous Party" in a way that it will never be sung again. Visitors from across the Atlantic whose sole vocal contribution was as part of a chorus of "Happy Birthday" at the end made unexpected appearances and curtsied to the box throughout the small hours. Dame Edith Evans, the famous early bird, blew kisses upwards from a seated position onstage, said that she remembered Noël from his boyhood and sat through to the very end. John Gielgud recalled his first employment in the theatre as Noël's understudy.

At the bar during the interval a man I didn't know greeted me warmly and said, "If a bomb were to fall here tonight, the English theatre would be wiped out for a generation to come."

If it was a night for rejoicing it was also a sentimental excursion down memory lane. There were not many youthful faces in evidence, and the audience as a whole had a stately look, unassailably correct and affirmatively mature. There were few of the great couturiers' novelties worn and the latest coiffure from Paris was not to be seen; everyone was formally but inconspicuously dressed. The spectacle was onstage and not in the stalls.

As the hours marched on, and one legendary talent succeeded another in the birthday offering, the mass emotion expressed itself as a general feeling of regret, a wistful sadness that seemed to say that nothing could ever be the same again, all true excellence as defined by the Coward era had vanished forever never to return.

The past was suddenly a tangible thing, to be recaptured there, in the middle of the night, as in some highly colored dream, grasped and savored and then permitted to vanish into history.

Tears were appropriate and tears flowed. Kay Hammond, the original Elvira of *Blithe Spirit*, in enforced retirement because of a crippling illness, was present in a white satin dress and managed to wave to Noël from her chair though the audience whispered that it believed her to be incapable of any movement at all. It was this gesture that triggered the general sniffling and brought out the handkerchiefs from pockets and purses, and their use throughout the night continued without embarrassment as others stepped out of the past and into the limelight one more time to pay homage to the Master.

I found myself remembering a remark Noël had once made to me in passing, in reference to a notably weepy performance by Mlle. Maria Casarès (regarded by an army of admirers, including me, as the world's greatest living actress), that tears were merely therapeutic, and quoted an old maxim about salt dissolved in water: its healing properties were to be found in the sweat of hard labor, at the seaside, and secreted in the tear duct, as well.

"There is nothing more satisfying in the theatre than a good cry," he added.

Only as the marathon matinee began to draw to a close were its pattern and meaning discernible: nearly a half century of English theatrical history had formed an orderly procession and marched before our eyes; nothing significant of Noël Coward's work was ignored, and even an untidy revue sketch from *This Year of Grace* was unearthed in the interests of thoroughness. Conceived as a tribute, the performance was a cavalcade, a dramatized biography of everyone present who was old enough to have been there when the parade started. The glass of fashion reflected the changing tastes of three royal reigns: Dame Edith wore lace and a choker of pearls that brought Queen Mary to mind, Dame Anna Neagle did a spirited Charleston in fringe and bugle beads. The balcony scene from *Private Lives* saw Elyot in the style of the thirties, wearing a white mess jacket and not a tuxedo; the distaff side, as the decades were spanned, identified the year we were meant to recall with the coiffure that was appropriate to it.

The theatre was host to the disembodied as well; everyone said so. On stage an impudent ghost invaded the body of a dancing girl so successfully that a well-remembered, if anonymous, beauty (one of Charles B. Cochran's line of "Young Ladies") was briefly restored to life, and the presence of Gertrude Lawrence hung in the air like a perfume she had worn. Never has a theatre entertained so many illustrious revenants all at once, summoned there by a thousand mediums and their affected memories.

History enacted by those who made it is stirring; it creates an appetite for more of the same, and the insatiable spectator is reluctant to give up his seat at the feast. The old show-business saying that it is always good to leave them wanting more was rarely better demonstrated than at the Phoenix that night: the cheering and the rhythmic clapping continued long after the royal party, who had initiated it, and then Noël himself had left the theatre.

The debonair young man with the heavy-lidded eyes and the insouciant manner, the matinee idol in the Charvet dressing gown who wrote daringly about adultery and sham, had begun his seventy-first year, and with it a new identity as the Grand Old Man of the Theatre. In fifteen days the New Year's Honors List would dub him a Knight Commander of the British Empire. Sheridan Morley's biography, *A Talent to Amuse,* was published that morning further to mark the milestone.

The critical brotherhood had almost never seen fit to disagree with his own view of his gifts: his was a "minor" or a "meager" talent; there was no depth in him, and no substance. There was diversion to be had from him, as there was diversion to be had from a game of charades at a country house party, and his tunes were nice enough if one happened to be on a dance floor when one heard them. There was facility to his dialogue, it was generally agreed, but it was never more than a surface, thin-as-ice aptitude, and some people were known to talk like characters in a Coward play, but characters in a Coward play never talked like the people one knew. Nor was there anything truly comic in his work; it was merely rather funny. His expertise in drawing a character swiftly and with few strokes was an acknowledged virtue, but that was no more than to be expected in the bag of tricks of a popular playwright. Moreover, there was an embarrassing and old-fashioned vein of sentimentality running through his mine that could not be overlooked. His narrative prose was a slavish imitation of Maugham's, another crowd-pleaser, and his only novel was a pastiche of Nancy Mitford out of Angela Thirkell. He had been a fine light comedian in earlier days, but his performances in later years were given mostly in cabarets, which showed a certain wisdom in his choice of venue. As an international pet of high society he had no equal, and in this milieu he was seen in his true perspective. And that was all there was to be said for Noël Coward.

The nocturnal matinee at the Phoenix Theatre wrote a full stop to that kind of professional criticism more emphatic than any exclamation point following a word of praise. It was time to have a fresh look at the work of five decades and see what might be hidden therein, a favorite pastime of critics and historians and academics in general. The archaeology was performed in a great rush, a kind of competitive dash to get into print the newest perceptions before the rivals did. One of Noël's friends recalled that a full moon had been shining at the time of the birthday nocturne and added a bit of farmer's wisdom: that a full moon always brings with it a decided change in the weather.

All the critics were evidently habitués of the night with fifty pounds to spend for the pleasure of it: the gala had been attended by everyone with space to fill and an article to write. The "historical" nature of the occasion informed their message to a man, and by week's end Noël Coward's true role had been identified as that of a "social historian" and spokesman for the Jazz Age, with additional insights relative to the decades that followed it. That this much had been clear to enlightened readers and theatregoers for a considerable time in no way diminished the gush of enthusiastic prose that proclaimed the news a real discovery of genuine importance. The noun "style" took on a meaning it had not worn since the days of Wilde, and the term "well-made play" was restored to respectability overnight. The critics found insistent echoes of Coward in many of the newer dramatists: Osborne, having long before said nice things about the Master's work, and Edward Albee, having written an introduction to a collection of Coward plays published in America, were both suddenly understood to be his direct heirs, and even Harold Pinter was, however unnecessarily, made into a branch of the family tree.

There was really very little else for the taste-makers to do. Everywhere one looked there was evidence of the Grand Old Man. Sean Kenny, the scenic designer and wit who distrusted everything that had happened in the world until the day before yesterday and was one of Noël's particular detractors, looked up from an appreciation of Coward in the Sunday *Observer* and remarked, "Oh, why don't they just make him an honorary member of the royal family and let us get on with something else!"

Dad's renaissance erupted all over the place: while the forward-looking theatrical managements in London and New York competed for the services of Vanessa Redgrave, Maggie Smith and other stellar ladies for revivals of *Private Lives* and *Design for Living,* a grammar school in Oxfordshire put on an amateur production of *Post-Mortem,* written in 1930 and never performed professionally. A London drama critic made it his business to review it and found it stocked with youthful excesses but "full of feeling."

Nearly completely forgotten was that Bernard Shaw had taken him seriously as long ago as 1921 and had written him a letter advising him to persevere, with the request that he never again read or see a Shaw play for fear of starting out as a "back number"; and Arnold Bennett introduced a volume of three plays with a complaint that the critics were wantonly irrational in their attitude towards Coward, listing three reasons for their hostility: the much-advertised speed with which the plays were written, the huge financial rewards accruing to a man who was still then in his twenties, and his choice of subjects. Bennett found his characters a "sad lot," and fundamentally lacking in civility, but acknowledged their existence in the real life of the English aristocracy among whom the author moved so easily. There was a strong implication in Bennett's heated defense of Noël the man and Coward the author that the critics were a jealous fraternity and resented the success of a young man from the lower middle class who was on friendly terms with the Prince of Wales and friendlier terms with all of Mayfair, where formal dress counted more than decorum.

If the critics had frequently been a thorn in Noël's side, the discomfort they produced was almost always accompanied by laughter, or at least an expression of pained amusement. He dismissed many of them as "journalists," when it was writers for the popular press who had attacked him, and the loftier practitioners of the form in the intellectual weeklies were dignified as "dusty dons" and "pale old professors" when they pronounced his entertainments insufficient to their aesthetic requirements. He often said, and in a way that admitted of no argument, that all his greatest successes had been uniformly badly reviewed, but this observation was highly inaccurate and was addressed, more often than not, to young authors and directors in need of comfort after a set of bad notices of their own. Two of the century's most learned critics of the drama, St. John Ervine and James Agate, were given to panegyrics when dealing with his early work and to reproaches later on; for them, Coward showed no development after *Cavalcade.*

"That word 'develop' is like a flag to a bull when I see it," he told me once. "Critics use it indiscriminately. I once saw it applied to a play of Shaw's—it may have been *Heartbreak House*—it was as if the old man were suffering from arrested growth of some kind. They always seem to be urging one to write like someone else, whereas a playwright who knows his business tries more and more to polish up his individuality and write in his own style that has served him well in the past. One of these days they will suggest that Harold Pinter has not 'developed,' whereas the opposite is true. His is quite the most unique talent I have ever come across, totally unlike any writer before him, and the style becomes more highly personal with each new thing he does.

"Looking over the past, I see all kinds of things I ought to have done very differently, errors of judgment that were the result of the *me* I was *then.* One play in particular was written out of the innocent desire to create two whopping good parts for the Lunts, which I did, and failed to write a good enough story to show off these parts. The result was half-hearted, neither comedy nor tragedy, and not skillful. The development that is wanted by all of us is the growth in skill, in handling one's materials with the art that conceals art, in economy of language, and not, I think, in our choice of themes.

"It has always seemed to me to be the business of comedy to hold the mirror up to the foibles of humanity—vanity, prejudice, sexual confusion, and so on. These were the materials of comic writers since the time of Aristophanes. If comedy is also useful in bringing about social change, that is all to the good. Since I first began to write plays, the world has changed considerably, but not in the least bit because of them. The two women getting drunk in the second act of *Fallen Angels* was, in 1923, so shocking to a certain part of the public that it was considered an outrage on all womanhood. The same situation in a play nowadays would be tame and reminiscent of a hundred others and leave its author open to the charge of imitativeness.

"I think I *have* developed and that my work shows it, if only to me. *A Song at Twilight* is far and away the best-constructed play I have ever written, and when I played it I knew as an actor that as a writer I had served myself very well; there is an almost mathematical precision to it that in no way detracts from the reality of it. It is the first play I have written whose theme was not attacked in at least one quarter as being flimsy or superficial."

The festivities of Holy Week were not so joyous as to prevent speculations from one and all about the precise state of Noël's health. There were rumors that he had been to see the renowned Dr. Niehans in Switzerland for a series of rejuvenating implantations whose effectiveness on the appearance and general health of a number of aging film stars was widely acknowledged. Noël admitted to having had one such subcutaneous injection but said that its principal effect was to have made him very sleepy, and added that the regime at the Niehans clinic, which banned smoking and alcohol for a period of three months, would improve anybody's appearance, as all forms of abstention invariably did.

Somebody said that when he was at home in Montreux he did nothing but lie in bed all day and consume chocolates, and he replied, "I also manage to solve any number of difficult crossword puzzles." But the impression was abroad that all creative work had ceased, that the writing of the third volume of his autobiography had been abandoned, and that he was too ill to continue with even the most modest undertaking.

Sheridan Morley's biography was widely read and much praised for its gentle understanding and delicacy in capturing an elusive personality so deftly in print. Its final chapter commenced with a rubric of Coward's own words:

"It's terrifying how little time there is left; every day now is a dividend, and there is still so much I want to do . . . but my life up to now has left me with no persistent regrets of any kind. I don't look back in anger, nor, indeed, in anything approaching even mild rage; I rather look back in pleasure and amusement. As for death, it holds no fear for me . . . provided it is not going to be a painful, lingering affair."

He said much the same thing to me in a short talk we had one afternoon in his suite at the Savoy; I am unable to recall, much as I have tried to, the correct placement of this in time, and my notebook provides no clue to set it with any degree of precision on the calendar of our meetings. The details are clear: there was a winter or an autumn sun sending a teatime refraction of yellowish light upwards from the Thames, slanting down the alley and invading the sitting room to make irregular patches on the carpet. He was wearing a dressing gown of some kind of Oriental silk and a printed foulard was knotted at his throat. The mandarin of earlier days smiled his Mahatma smile and put the best face on things that he could manage. There seemed to be something the matter with his dental occlusion.

Cole Lesley had poured out cups of tea, solicited news of my activities as I inquired of his in return, and left us to go on an errand for the Master. Someone of great theatrical eminence had died in America and the obituaries in newsprint were folded back the easier for Noël to read them; then he looked up again with a look of bewilderment and sadness and removed the spectacles.

"Une autre tranche dans ma route," he said. To say in French that another grave had been dug in his path was much more than I wanted to hear; the cemeteries had already received so many of those he had known and loved and helped. The death of Lorne Lorraine, his secretary for forty-seven years, who had been both a friend and a boss and sometimes even a motherly aunt, had affected him greatly; there had been a long and painful illness that preceded it, and Mrs. Lorraine, by all accounts, had endured it with a toughness of spirit that one close observer described as "unequivocally dignified."

"Of course, we all know that I shouldn't smoke and they've all been at me for years to stop," he said, in some effort to apologize for the fact that his hand trembled with the weight of the teacup, "but I simply cannot *not* smoke. The psychiatrists all talk about the need for oral satisfaction and I suppose they're right, but even a conscious determination to cut down is a deprivation instead."

I said something to the effect that if one had been smoking for many years it didn't seem much use to stop, then realized that what was unspoken was the idea of there being so little time left, and saw that he realized the implication as well. He launched into his little speech then, enumerating the regrets he didn't have and naming his specific blessings; it had the sound of having been prepared beforehand and even of having benefited from rehearsal: its purpose was to put visitors at their ease, and it succeeded admirably in this aim. There was a kind of relaxed gallantry in the way he said it, almost frivolously, and the word "amusement" occurred at least twice, drawn out in such a way as to suggest just how extensive the pleasure had been. And then the subject was dropped, as if exhausted, and the attention shifted to me.

He wanted to know what I was reading, always a matter of interest to him, and I said I was in the middle of Nabokov's *Ada* and having a splendid time with it.

"He's a neighbor of mine in Switzerland," he remarked, as if this constituted his entire acquaintance with the novelist.

I told him about an interview Nabokov had given to the BBC in which all the questions to be asked him had been submitted a long time in advance and to which all his answers were magnificently and wittily prepared, and Noël, raising his eyebrows, pronounced it an excellent idea. Nabokov had dismissed with faint praise some of the literary giants of this century and the last, calling Henry James a "mere gossip" and saying of the author of a book he called *The Karamazov Brothers* that he revealed very little familiarity with Russian life. Noël was delighted to hear about this, and his shoulders shook with laughter; impudence *from* great men rather than to them always met with his approval. The inversion of the words in the title of the Dostoevsky novel delighted him, and I thought I saw his mind working over possible variations on a theme: *The Sisters Three,* perhaps, or an equivalent; but instead he observed, reasonably, that it was likely the work had been translated into French before coming into English and that the French title, *Les Frères Karamazoff,* had established its rhythm in the translator's ear.

He had seen and admired a film for which Harold Pinter wrote the screenplay, and he embarked once more on his almost passionate lecture on the author's rare gifts, singling him out from other contemporaries whose work he found drab and lacking in theatrical skill. He particularly disliked a play that season that had sent the critics into performing cartwheels over its novelty and excellence. "It is merely modish," he said, "and there is nothing in this world more old-fashioned than modishness. Nowadays the characters are so brutally unkind to each other, not merely flippantly rude, as they used to be in drawing room comedies. The hostilities are all exposed like a nerve, and it makes me, for one, decidedly uncomfortable watching them.

"And now there's the nudity, which is all right at the Folies Bergère. I mean, one can spend several weeks in Paris and if you are clever *not* go to the Folies Bergère. In *Hair,* as Jack Benny said, the nude scene was so brief one hadn't time to notice if any of the actors were Jewish, but the *Oh, Calcutta!* people make one feel you are in a Turkish bath, and they are all so physically unimpressive. Really, fifteen acorns are hardly worth the price of admission."

He returned to the subject of kindness later, wondering at its disappearance from the everyday behavior of one's associates at work and play. He thought its notable absence was in some way connected with the seeming inability of the young to express love, as if the noblest of emotions were now a matter for shame and embarrassment, and he struggled to make emphatic the difference between love as he understood it and sexual passion or mere sentiment, and uttered again the word "kindness" like something in a foreign language he was trying to express in English.

Kenneth Tynan, writing in the *Observer* the week after Noël died, recalled an instance of the Master's specific kindness to him.

It had occurred at the time when Tynan was writing drama criticism for *The New Yorker* and on the evening of the day when a particularly demolishing review he had written of a Coward production appeared in print. He was dining alone in Sardi's, nearly always empty during the middle of the evening, only to see Noël, also alone, at another table. Tynan knew him only slightly, but Noël spotted him and padded across the room to the table behind which Tynan says he was "cringing." Noël applied a four-letter expletive to him, smiled, and said, "Come and have dinner with me!"

Tynan was limp with relief and joined him at his table. Noël talked of many things, of the nature of the writer's ego, of his own pride, of the perilous state of the theatre and particularly of Tynan's own career, never once mentioning the bad review in *The New Yorker* or the show it had assailed. "It would have been easy to cut or crush me," wrote the critic, "but it was typical of Coward that he chose, with an almost certain flop on his hands, to amuse and advise me instead." It was, indeed, "typical" of Coward, if at complete variance with what those who didn't know him would have expected to be "typical" in the given situation. The general and popular impression of him had been nourished by gossips and other devotees of funny lines, scandal and bitchery that he was charming and cruel in about equal measure, that the company of his peers was the only possible companionship for him, especially if those peers were internationally celebrated, and that his own celebrity had been achieved not so much by his acting, writing or composing as by his gift for the devastating remark.

The snappy rejoinder and the quip with the finely honed edge always achieve a wider circulation by far than expressions of encouragement or praise no matter how felicitously made, and the nature of laughter is such that what is funniest and worthiest of quotation usually has a deflating motive at its center. It would be untrue to affirm that what one remembers best of Noël's conversation was that which was most expressive of his generosity and kindness, or that the evidence of his loving nature outweighed everything that was quirky and sharply critical in his pronouncements. Yet it is oddly true that his admiring words for others are the ones that many cherish most. I can never think of Mary Martin without recalling Noël's expression of wonder at the effect she had on him in the theatre: "She alarms and delights me almost unbearably." George Grizzard, who retains the same look of an undergraduate he had when he first walked on a Broadway stage twenty years ago, thinks the finest compliment he ever had was Noël's: "You are the funniest old man I have ever seen on a stage." And Vivien Leigh feigned puzzlement and even distress when repeating what the Master had said: "He says that even my *hair* is made of porcelain, when it *isn't,* you know."

Praising the novel I had written, in a letter to me sent in care of Elaine Stritch, he wrote, "I am sending this in care of my favorite wage-earner because I do not now know where you live, or even *how* you live. I only know *why* you live, and that is to be a bloody good writer." The Cockneyism rescued the compliment from the mundane.

That afternoon at the Savoy, as I sat among lengthening shadows and half-empty teacups, an ineffable sadness seized me; the "pathetic fallacy," so much despised by dramatists, was strongly operative: a wintry wind coursed down the alleyway from the Thames. An implicit message of finality reached me: we had first met in strong sunlight and were now perhaps bidding each other farewell in the approaching dusk. He seemed tired, even exhausted, and I knew it was time to take my leave. We shook hands and exchanged broad smiles a shade too hearty to carry real conviction, and when I found myself outside the hotel and walking in the Strand I could only recall his words at the funicular station on Capri: *"Partir, c'est mourir un peu,"* which I kept running over in my mind like rosary beads, until they were displaced by other words of French, those of La Fontaine: "Death never takes the wise man by surprise; he is always ready to go."

We saw each other once more at a splendid party given in his honor only a few weeks before his life ended; the grand-gala evening marked his first visit to a charming and intimate presentation of his songs in revue form, "Oh, Coward!" which had been delighting New York audiences for months. Admission to the performance that Sunday evening was by invitation only, and at the end of it, when the cheering had died and the lights in the auditorium were put out, the audience moved in taxis and limousines to a vast restaurant on the ground floor of a skyscraper whose name promised simple Roman fare in a casual setting. Instead, the supper was sumptuous, and the decor afforded no more than a mute background for the showy gathering. Noël, his stoop giving him the look of someone in perpetual search for a dropped object in his path, came with Marlene Dietrich, who offered strong support and a cheery smile as he made his slow and difficult passage to the table of honor.

It was generally agreed that New York had not experienced a party like it in decades, and a current of nostalgia flowed unchecked from one celebrant to another like a heady contagion. All the newest finery was on display and some of the oldest: there were guests in evidence who had not been seen publicly, at least at night, for ten years or more, and it was reassuring to see that those presumed dead were, in reality, ostentatiously quick. Not merely splendor gave the occasion its tone and dignity: the elite of show business in all its manifestations had rarely been so concentrated in one place at the same time, and only one theatrical giant could have summoned them there to do him honor. One of them remarked upon the restoration of elegance to New York life, and all agreed that it had been absent for too long, but then only Noël Coward had the magnitude to revive it, however briefly, and lure the really "right" people out of their dim cloisters and into the light again. Another man, with an international reputation for spitefulness and exaggerated self-esteem, observed wistfully that an era had most certainly reached its conclusion on the glittering occasion but that the gallant gentlefolk who attended it showed a great nobility of feeling in behaving as though nothing could ever come to an end. He also noted the absence of gate-crashers and news photographers and applauded the sophistication of the hosts in their seating arrangements. It made the inevitable game of musical chairs, customarily played at evenings of this kind, so much more gracefully possible, he thought, and the placement of Noël's table in a far corner was a stroke of imaginative genius, permitting a kind of receiving line to form all by itself without reference to priorities of rank, its sole object a private need to greet the Master personally with expressions of love.

Noël sat through it all benignly and with exquisite patience, murmuring to each new arrival at his side that he had loved the evening's entertainment, that he had left the show "whistling the tunes," that, yes, he was off in a day or so to Jamaica to get some sun. Winners of gilded Hollywood statuettes a generation earlier stood in long dresses like obedient schoolgirls about to be presented to the Dean, each preserving an unchallenged identity that did not admit of reintroduction ("Hello, Noël, how long it's been! Let me say hello to Marlene, too!"), and once-eminent impresarios in tuxedos green with wear steadied themselves on canes as they waited their turn.

Three vacant places at Noël's table accommodated a series of tentative visits from old friends, asked to sit down "for a minute" by Cole Lesley until their designated occupants, the three performers of the evening's entertainment, should appear to claim them. One of those favored was Leonard Lyons, recovered from a long illness, along with his gracious wife; they and Noël gossiped amiably, reminding each other of amusements shared long ago in the company of vanished friends. Mrs. Lyons and I replayed, as is our custom, the scene of a chance meeting we had years ago when I surprised her at the scrutiny of a rosebush in the Great Hall at Harrod's, and we laughed extravagantly, as people always do at a fond memory; still, her attention was not fully on me, nor mine on her. She kept a nanny's eye on Leonard, alert for signs of fatigue, and included Noël in this supervision, as though they were charges being permitted to stay up long past their bedtime.

And still they came, the faces from the past, figures from a theatrical scrapbook, to offer a hand that said hello and a fixed smile betraying that what was really meant was "adieu." The Master received each one in kind, as do certain members of English royalty, with a blend of the familiar and the formal, as if shaking hands with an old and valued acquaintance whose name could not instantly be recalled to mind. The strain of it was painful to observe. The demands of what he had always called "urbanity" were now unendurable, yet the smile continued and the welcoming words were bestowed on all comers with the same degree of enthusiasm and joy. There were those he had never met who came to announce the fact, to identify themselves and express their gratitude for the contribution he had made to their lives. One man said he merely wanted "to thank Santa Claus for everything," and the brevity of the remark earned him a special smile. Mrs. Lyons said to me in an undertone, "Can't they *see* how tired he is?" We managed, he and I, to have no more than a few words together,

246

and, as always, his were ones of encouragement. Soon it was possible for him to withdraw, to cross the restaurant a step at a time supported on both sides, to rest for a moment in a straight-backed chair before being helped into his coat, as the party averted its eyes from his difficulty. I stood near the outer door to see him leave, my emotions identical to those I had felt at the Queen's Theatre when he spoke the curtain line, "Good night, sweetheart." He grimaced at the awkwardness of his exit, and stepped into a patch of wet on the sidewalk, leaving a firm moist print on the dry concrete with each footfall of his passage to the waiting car. When the car had moved away, I stood in the January chill looking at the odd, wet pattern of his steps and thinking that I had never noticed before that his feet were really quite large.

Eight weeks later the expected news reached me via telephone: his death had been sudden, in the early morning, at his home in Jamaica; the fact was incontrovertible, but the details vague. I went to the newsroom of a television network and watched yellow paper issue from the Telex machine, searching for specifics among the Wall Street quotations and the results of far-flung football matches: bits and pieces of obituary material rolled upwards in repetitive confusion, odds and ends of half-truths and wire-service surmises. Item by item, interspersed with unwelcome trivia from the money market and the playing fields, the history of a friend moved into view on the roller, couched in the language of journalism he so despised; fact after lifeless fact, irrelevant date after inaccurate attribution of authorship, the record rolled past.

I left the newsroom with a strong sense of disorientation: one more plane of existence had been displaced by another, unfamiliar one; one more treasured habit was broken—a fine habit, *my* habit, the habit of friendship with Noël Coward. This was no mere instance of another *tranche dans ma route;* greater than the sense of a directionless path ahead was my astonishment at the absence of affect I felt at the realization he was dead. I knew that the man with the extraordinary gift of applying his own quotation marks to much of what he had to say had left behind more than the treasure of his words and music. The heritage was far greater than what could be performed on a stage in revival or played and replayed on phonographs or by the dance bands of luxury hotels around the world.

I walked from the television skyscraper towards the Broadway theatre district in a swirl of snowflakes, odd, irrelevant memories of Noël dancing about in my head as the flurry developed into a serious and steady fall of snow. I crossed Broadway at 53rd Street as the sky darkened in the baleful way that so often tells of a coming blizzard. New Yorkers know that darkness at noon presages inconveniences later in the day; theatre managers think only of the box-office receipts for the evening performance. In the nearly vain hope that business will not fall off because of the weather, they throw the switches and illuminate their marquees. As I stiffened against the icy precipitation, the Broadway Theatre turned on its lights. Beyond it, a sign advertising a new musical comedy at a newly built theatre flickered into the midday gloom.

I didn't want to think about funerals, or memorial services, or travel accommodations made in a great hurry to attend one or the other. I felt, urgently, that the only appropriate thing to do was to go to the box office and buy a ticket to see an entertainment performed by live actors before an audience that had paid for its tickets. The new theatre was near at hand, a revolutionary design in a glass and steel tower that included as part of the complex a restaurant and drinking establishment called the Pub Theatrical. The shortest direct route to the theatre's box office was through a long corridor that joined the restaurant to the outer lobby of the theatre, and I chose to take it rather than an alternative one in the falling snow. The corridor was lined then, as it is today, with huge weathered lithographs advertising turn-of-the-century theatres and Sarah Bernhardt's farewell American tour, together with blown-up photographs of the theatrical elite of a later day. At the very end of the passage, a few steps from the door that connects it to the theatre proper, an enlarged likeness of Noël, a light-colored raincoat thrown over the shoulders of his dinner jacket, beamed outwards with a look of cheery surprise, as if he had not expected a camera to be anywhere nearby. I looked at it for a while, and finally smiled back at it.

And, once again encouraged to "get on with it," I proceeded directly to the box office and bought tickets for that evening's performance.